POPULISM

POPULISM

Reaction or Reform?

Edited by THEODORE SALOUTOS

University of California, Los Angeles

HOLT, RINEHART AND WINSTON

New York · Chicago · San Francisco · Atlanta
Dallas · Montreal · Toronto · London

Cover illustration: "A Party of Patches. Grand Balloon Ascension, Cincinnati, May 20th, 1891." Among the Populist leaders in the balloon basket are Terence V. Powderly and "Sockless" Jerry Simpson. Cartoon by Bernhard Gillam appearing on the cover of *Judge*, June 6, 1891. (*The Granger Collection*)

CONTENTS

"Candidate Billy's Busy Day." William Jennings Bryan is shown in this cartoon as having accepted the nomination of the Populist, Free Silver, and Democratic parties. Pen and ink drawing by G. Y. Coffin, September 13, 1896. (*Library of Congress*)

INTRODUCTION

The Populists occupy a unique place in American history because they comprised the first third party of significance to challenge the Republican and Democratic parties. By challenging the two major parties the Populists reaffirmed their faith in political democracy and expressed confidence in the belief that a new party, freed from the corruptive influences of the old, would be more receptive to the needs of the people. This challenge brought the Populists to the forefront of the reform movement that swept the country during the closing decades of the nineteenth century. As in the case of other reform parties, the Populists served as a rallying point for various smaller protest groups that sought to identify themselves with what they expected would become a mighty political force.

Especially to the hard-pressed farmers of the South and Middle West, the time seemed ripe for political action. Agriculture still was the dominant occupation in the country, but its position was being threatened as the times changed. The spread of industrial capitalism, the rise of cities, the growth of financial institutions, the influx of new immigrants, the passing of the era of cheap lands, the fear of trusts and monopolies, and the maldistribution of wealth were viewed as threats to the life and values of a rural America. Sweeping social changes were altering the social structure of the country and relegating the farmers to a subordinate position in society. At the same time the farmers began to feel that the earlier crusades to obtain fair treatment from the railroads, to regulate the trusts, to establish cooperatives, and in general to raise the prices of farm products were not bringing them the relief they sought. The formation of a new political party seemed to offer them a speedier and more effective means of obtaining relief.

The Populist party was, for the most part, a party of farmers and townspeople with a rural orientation, and to a much lesser extent of wage earners, single-taxers, members of the professional classes, preachers, prohibitionists, suffragettes, and other reformers. The argument was that farmers had to elect farmers and their allies to office, as these had first-hand knowledge of the needs of the farmers and could be relied upon to enact legislation beneficial to their interests.

Within recent years the role of the Populists in American history has become a subject of spirited debate. One group believes that the Populists were a positive and constructive force and that they contributed to the American heritage of freedom and democracy. This interpretation of Populism has been effectively stated by John D. Hicks in *The Populist Revolt* (1931). Another group of scholars questions this interpretation and counters with the charge that the earlier historian failed to bring out the antisocial and negative features of Populism. The readings presented here give the arguments of both groups, so as to enable the student to judge for himself whether Populism was a positive or a negative force, and whether it was related to twentieth-century reform movements.

Among those portraying a sympathetic understanding of the background, aims, and tactics of the Populists is Eric F. Goldman. The first selection, taken from his writings, provides an abbreviated but pointed introduction to the Populists and their programs. Goldman lays bare the fears of the doctrinaire group that banded together under the Populist banner to defend themselves from presumed exploiters who threatened their rise on the economic ladder. The complaints and demands of this group made many angry, and even caused liberals to cry out in protest against some of the Populist proposals.

In the years following the collapse of the Populist movement in 1896, few scholars gave it serious thought. Political action among the farmers was discredited for a number of years. Hence the demands of the agriculturalists in the immediate post-Populist period assumed an economic rather than a political character. Farmers' organizations avoided politics and concentrated their efforts on campaigns to reduce the acreage of wheat and cotton, to hold these crops off the market for higher prices, and to seek better credit facilities. Furthermore, the return of better times for farmers and the emergence of other domestic issues and problems growing out of World War I tended to lessen the concern of historians with agrarian issues.

A series of social and political events brought new meaning to Populism during the Progressive era, even though scholarly interest in it at the time was minimal. The accomplishments under Woodrow Wilson's New Freedom were more in line with the objectives of the Populists and more helpful than the legislation passed during the administration of Theodore Roosevelt. The income tax, one of the Populist proposals, became law. The Federal Warehouse Act of 1916, which made it possible for farmers to store their products at reasonable rates, was a partial realization of the Populist demand for the subtreasury plan; and the Federal Farm Loan Act of 1916 furnished mortgage facilities that were unavailable during the heyday of Populism.

With the prolonged farm crisis after World War I, the oncoming of the Great Depression of the 1930s, and the beginning of the New Deal in 1933, Populist principles assumed even greater significance. The demands to vest greater authority in the federal government to combat the depression, provide farmers with cheaper and more abundant credit, inflate the currency, increase the purchasing power of the masses, and place more effective curbs on finance, industry, and commerce were in keeping with proposals of the most ardent Populists. The philosophical and psychological bond between the New Deal and Populism was real. At no time were the underlying principles of Populism accepted with greater enthusiasm than during the years of the New Deal.

The next three selections appeared shortly before or after the launching of the New Deal. It should be noted that while John D. Hicks is a historian, Roscoe C. Martin a political scientist, and David Saposs an economist, all three agree that Populism had a socially constructive influence.

The selection by John D. Hicks is a neat synthesis of the research that went into *The Populist Revolt*. It focuses attention on the role of farmers and wage earners, analyzes the influence the passing of the era of cheap and free lands had on the rise of Populism, explains why the Populists sought the assistance of the federal government and what they wanted from it, and discusses the persistence of the movement after the collapse of the party structure. According to Hicks, the Populists anticipated and diagnosed some of the major political and economic ills of the day, problems that have haunted succeeding generations. Further, he argues that the Populists were committed to the public interest and were not narrow and self-centered as their contemporaries portrayed them. In a broader context, Populism was more than an agrarian revolt. Hicks refrains from drawing a hard-and-fast line between farmers and wage earners.

Roscoe C. Martin's study of the Populists in Texas appeared during the first year of the New Deal. Although Martin reinforces Hicks's arguments, his emphasis is different. Hicks stresses the long-range observations that interest the historian; Martin, the more immediate problems that interest the political scientist. What were these problems?

Besides analyzing the problems facing a new party in a one-party state, Martin discusses the indebtedness of the Texas Populists to Thomas Jefferson, the Greenbackers, and the Farmers' Alliance, and finds that they drew support from ranchers, farmers, workingmen, and periodically from Republicans, Socialists, and Prohibitionists. The party members often consulted the Bible as the final authority. Of special interest were their labors among the foreign-born and the Negroes. The confused and clumsy Texas Populists had a reformist influence on the Democratic party. What was the nature of that influence?

David Saposs analyzes Populism in terms of middle-class attitudes and behavior, and in some respects anticipates a part of the revisionist argument of the 1950s. His point of view differs from that of Hicks and of Martin in that it revolves around the liberal political thinking of the 1930s, which reflected the influences of Populism. Saposs concerns himself more with the Populist rationale that percolated down into the 1930s than with Populist thought in the 1890s. He calls attention to the rise of several political movements: the Non-Partisan League in North Dakota, which accepted the underlying philosophy of the Populists favoring broader federal authority but preferred to work from within one of the major parties; the Minnesota Farmer-Labor Party; and the Progressive party, launched by Robert M. La Follette in 1924. The rise of such movements was to him evidence of the persistence of Populist influence after the defeat of 1896. His incisive comments do not obscure the negative side of Populism, which he also brings out.

Saposs sees something in the future of the Populist heritage that no scholar prior to his time had mentioned: it could easily take an undemocratic turn and assume the dimensions of totalitarianism. This could happen because the United States, at the time he was writing, was experiencing the worst depression in history. Saposs describes those elements in American society which he thinks were susceptible to Populist thought, classifies what he considers were the three types of Populism, and finally identifies certain prototypes of American fascism. Which politicians of the 1930s does he place in these categories and equate with their counterparts of the 1890s?

Jack Abramowitz, in the next selection, treats a much-ignored phase of the movement by observing that the Populists made a heroic effort to resolve the racial question. The student would do well to observe the states in which the Populists sought to cooperate with the Negroes, the extent of the progress made in each state, and the effect the collapse of Populism had on Negroes. More significant are the reasons why the Negroes identified themselves with the Populists.

The selections from Saposs and Abramowitz indicate that the Populists were more modern in their outlook than many realized. Whereas Saposs emphasizes the democratic features of Populism and suggests that they could be diverted in the direction of totalitarianism, Abramowitz focuses attention on Populist efforts to bring about Negro participation in the political life of the nation. The concern with totalitarianism in the 1930s and civil rights during the 1950s and 1960s helps give Populism a current flavor.

Scholars were critical of the Populists from the beginning. The earlier critics found fault with their analysis of the money question, their crusade for regulation of railroads, and their demand for more federal controls; while critics of the 1950s and 1960s concentrated on the negative and antisocial aspects of Populism. The earlier critics were more concerned with issues as a matter of public policy, while the later ones confined themselves to the realm of academic debate.

One of the early critics was Frank LeRond McVey, an economist and inveterate foe of the Populists, who wrote a monograph about them in 1896. McVey was disturbed about the paternalistic features of Populism, which he equated with socialism. He viewed reliance on the government as retrogressive and hence a negative force in the development of the country. Even more regrettable to him was the nurturing of what he considered to be the Populist brand of socialism on American soil.

Anna Rochester, writing in the 1940s, views Populism from still another perspective. She compares the radical American tradition of the 1940s with the past and identifies Populism with earlier protest movements in the United States. Note whom she considers the outstanding heir of Populism in World War II and compare her interpretation with that of McVey.

Essays critical of Hicks's interpretation made their appearance during the 1950s and 1960s. The next two selections were inspired by conditions growing out of the conservative reaction associated with Senator Joseph R. McCarthy, whose home state of Wisconsin has been closely identified with the liberal agrarian tradition. The social and political climate under which these essays were written differed sharply from that under which Hicks, Martin, and Saposs wrote.

The first historian to challenge Hicks's interpretation was Richard Hofstadter. In "The Folklore of Populism," the essay that ignited the controversy and which contains the essence of his argument, Hofstadter weighs what he considers to be the contributions and weaknesses of Populism. He concludes that the latter outweigh the former and asks for a reappraisal of the movement. Hofstadter's arguments are directed more at Hicks than at Martin simply because Hicks's impact has been greater. Students should study the validity of Hofstadter's arguments supporting his evaluations of the Populists. He makes much of the "soft" side of Populism and argues that the Populists were looking back to a golden past. He stresses anti-Semitism among the Populists. What evidence does he present in support of the charge? The Hofstadter argument in the final analysis quickened the interest in Populism.

Victor C. Ferkiss is more revisionist than Hofstadter. He is a political scientist who insists that Populism was a forerunner of American fascism. The student would find it rewarding to reread the section of the Saposs article that deals with prototypes of American fascism and see how far beyond Saposs Ferkiss goes. Among the highly debatable views Ferkiss, writing in 1957, raises are the following: the Populist rationale was dealt a deathblow by World War II; monetary reform is dead as an issue; the farmers are more interested in price supports than in reforms; and the surviving American Populists have been swallowed up by the "radical right."

Among the first scholars to reply to the attacks against the standard interpretation of the Populists was C. Vann Woodward. He concedes that the leading writers of the 1930s and the 1940s accepted the Hicks interpretation without much question and that the McCarthy era caused scholars such as Hofstadter and Ferkiss to concentrate on anti-Semitism, antiforeignism, nationalism, and other antisocial phases believed to have been a part of Populism. He finds a positive and negative side to Populism, much to applaud and something to condemn. He raises other questions, too, that have concerned serious students of Populism. For instance, he asks whether the Middle West was a greater repository of Populism than the South? Were the Populists the perpetrators or the victims of bigotry and the lynch spirit? He finds it difficult to follow the reasoning of those who link Populism with fascism.

Another scholar who takes issue with the revisionist position, especially that of Ferkiss, is William P. Tucker. He finds that the analogies "between American fascism and [the] assumed characteristics of American populism" are somewhat overdrawn. His views of Populism in relation to finance capitalism, the right of labor to organize, civil liberties, foreign policy, and anti-Semitism differ sharply from those of Ferkiss.

Still another reply to the revisionists is provided by Walter T. K. Nugent, in his account of a study to determine the attitude of the Populists to the foreign-born and their institutions in Kansas, and the extent to which the foreign-born participated in the Populist party. His findings in the foreign-language press and the local depositories of Kansas go a long way in answering the charges of antiforeignism and anti-Semitism.

Hicks, for the most part, has not attempted to answer his critics, but he has expressed himself on the general subject. In an article written in 1956 he reassesses "Our Pioneer Heritage," an article he wrote some thirty years earlier, which anticipated much of the thinking that went into *The Populist Revolt*. In the more recent article he explains what influenced him and other historians in the earlier period, and tells how he would have handled the same theme had he been writing in 1956. He indicates the issues on which he would have placed greater stress.

In the final section Theodore Saloutos examines the nature of the scholarly praise and criticism directed at the Populists before the revisionist attacks of the 1950s. He analyzes the nature of the early attacks and finds that the Populists came to be better appreciated when the proponents of the New Freedom came into office and later when the New Dealers took charge of the federal government. He likewise examines the principal arguments of the revisionists. The study supports the position of Hicks that Populism was a socially constructive force in American history.

In the reprinted selections footnotes appearing in the original sources have in general been omitted unless they contribute to the argument or better understanding of the selection.

ERIC F. GOLDMAN (b. 1915), Rollins Professor of
History at Princeton University, is representative of the
historians who treat Populism as part of the Progressive and
liberal tradition. A graduate of Johns Hopkins University
and author of *Rendezvous with Destiny* (1953), *Crucial
Decade* (1956), and other works, his liberal views and
persuasive style of writing and lecturing have had wide
appeal. Populism, according to Goldman, was a conspicuous
part of the broader reform movement that swept
late-nineteenth-century America. He finds that despite the
diversity of interests of the various Populist groups, they had
enough in common to unite under one banner. Populism
was more than an agrarian movement.*

Eric F. Goldman

A Least Common Denominator

With dissidence permeating both the
urban and rural regions, reformers naturally
dreamed of a national union of the discontented that would mean sure political power.
There were certainly plenty of encouraging
facts. Whatever their doctrinal differences,
the Farmers' Alliances, Knights of Labor,
socialists, single-taxers, even the anarchists,
were united by a fear of big business and by an
impatience with liberalism's refusal to
sanction governmental action in behalf of the
poor. Two local elections of the Eighties sent
a special thrill of hope through the coali-
tionists. In 1886, single-taxers, socialists,
union members, and thousands of citizens
who were just plain irritated supported

Henry George with such fervor that he barely
missed winning the mayorship of New York;
a rising young liberal named Theodore Roosevelt ran third.[1] Then, in the state and national elections of 1890, candidates backed by
the Alliances scored a series of striking victories in the South and West. Five United
States Senators, six Governors, and forty-six
Congressmen championing bold new economic legislation, a single-taxer almost
mayor of the nation's metropolis—weren't
these facts sure harbingers of a new national
party of urban and rural discontent, which
would take power as the coalition Republican
Party had triumphed in 1860? With the approach of the Presidential election of 1892,

more than thirteen hundred delegates converged on Omaha to get under way just such a coalition, the "People's" or "Populist" Party.

Hour after hour anger swept through the cavernous old Coliseum Building. July 1892 brought as wilting a heat as Omaha had ever known, the city frolicked in a Fourth-of-July mood, near-by saloons had laid in an extra supply of liquor. But nothing could distract the delegates from their rounds of furious speeches, wild applause, and fierce resolutions. From all parts of the United States, some bumping along hundreds of miles in buckboards, others using their last folding money for train fare, the Populists had gathered to launch an all-out assault on the political and economic masters of America. They did it with the dedicated wrath of a camp meeting warring on the Devil himself.

Any delegate who strayed from the mood of the convention was promptly hurled back on a wave of emotion. Midway in the proceedings a member of the Resolutions Committee, pointing out that the Union Pacific had not provided the reduced rates usually granted for convention delegates, proposed that the railroad should be asked to rectify this "oversight." Instantly Marion Cannon, of California, was on his feet, his face livid. An oversight? Ask a corporation to be fair? Cannon shouted. The "customary courtesy was denied deliberately and with insolence. I do not want this Convention. . .to go back to the railroad company, hat in hand, and ask for any privileges whatever. The Democrats and Republicans secured half-fare, but we— not connected with railroads, but producers of the earth—have been refused equal terms." The delegates thundered approval as Cannon concluded: "We can stand the refusal."[2]

On the afternoon of July 4, a plump, genial Irishman with a reputation for quips and politicking mounted the rostrum and this day he sounded like a prophet out of the Old Testament. "We meet in the midst of a nation brought to the verge of moral, political, and material ruin," Ignatius Donnelly cried. ". . . Corruption dominates the ballot-box, the Legislatures, the Congress, and touches even the ermine of the bench. . . . Our homes [are] covered with mortgages. . .the land [is] concentrating in the hands of the capitalists. The urban workmen are denied the rights of organization for self protection; imported, pauperized labor beats down their wages; a hireling standing army, unrecognized by our laws, is established to shoot them down, and they are rapidly degenerating into European conditions. A vast conspiracy against mankind has been organized. . . . If not met and overthrown at once it forebodes terrible social convulsions. . .or the establishment of an absolute despotism."[3]

This was the kind of language the delegates wanted to hear. When the specific proposals of the platform continued in the same tone, the convention exploded into a demonstration unprecedented in all the turbulent history of American political gatherings. With the last thrust at "tyranny and oppression," the delegates rose in a cheering, stomping, marching mass. Hats, coats, papers, fans, umbrellas went up in the air, leaders were bounced from shoulder to shoulder, every state tried to outdo the next in noise and movement. Texans whooped and beat on coffee cans. Nebraskans chanted: "What is home without a mortgage? Don't all speak at once." New Yorkers hoisted a beaming old man to the platform, thrust a baton in his hand, yelled wildly while he pretended to lead the musicians in hymns and marching songs. "Good-Bye, My Party, Good-Bye," the delegates sang. Then, to the tune of "Save a Poor Sinner, Like Me," they shouted how "the railroads and old party bosses together did sweetly agree" to deceive and exploit "a hayseed like me." And, breaking through the bedlam time and again, came the "People's

Hymn," sung to the consecrated music of the "Battle Hymn of the Republic":

They have stolen our money, have ravished our homes;
With the plunder erected to Mammon a throne;
They have fashioned a god, like the Hebrews of old,
Then bid us bow down to their image of gold.[4]

Edwin Godkin read the reports from Omaha and erupted in an editorial that was all anger and foreboding. Carl Schurz, proclaiming the Republic near "the precipice," poured out a thirty-four-page letter pleading for Cleveland's re-election. Theodore Roosevelt seized every opportunity to denounce the "wild Farmers' Alliance cranks."[5] In free-trade clubs, in universities, at soirées, wherever liberals gathered, the news from Omaha left men furious and frightened. Here was a drastically, alarmingly different reformism, bursting up from the bottom.

The leaders at Omaha made it emphatically plain that they intended to base their movement on the groups which the Best People were sure represented the worst people. Populism, almost the first words of the Omaha platform declared, was to be a "permanent and perpetual. . .union of the labor forces of the United States. . . . The interests of rural and civic [urban] labor are the same; their enemies are identical." Since the convention was predominantly agrarian, Populist leaders were careful to emphasize their interest in labor's problems, and resolutions adopted by the convention supported the most important labor demands of the day. The delegates condemned "the fallacy of protecting American labor under the present system, which opens our ports to the pauper and criminal classes of the world, and crowds out our wage earners"; cordially sympathized with the efforts of workingmen to shorten their hours of labor; and roundly denounced "the maintenance of a large standing army of mercenaries, known as the Pinkerton

system, as a menace to our liberties." No labor convention would have cared to improve on the language of a resolution that condemned "the recent invasion of the Territory of Wyoming by the hired assassins of Plutocracy, assisted by Federal officers."[6]

Another resolution provoked a debate which showed that these pro-labor statements were no mere contrivances on the part of leaders, slipped by an indifferent rank and file. While the convention met, a Knights of Labor union was engaged in a hard-fought strike against a group of Rochester clothing manufacturers, and the resolution not only expressed support of the strikers against a "tyrannical combine" but called on "all who hate tyranny and oppression" to boycott the goods of the manufacturers. Sympathy for strikers was one thing; a secondary boycott was going far (so far that its legality was decidedly in question). A secondary boycott was going much too far for a Texas delegate, who wanted to table the resolution, and for a New Yorker, who proposed dividing it so that he could vote for the sympathy and against the boycott.

Promptly, two of the most unmistakably agrarian delegates were on their feet in defense of the boycott. "There is no such thing as a boycott," roared "Cyclone" Davis, of Texas. "It only consists in letting your enemies alone and staying with your friends."

Then Ignatius Donnelly, from agricultural Minnesota, took up the fight. "If this resolution was simply to express our prejudice of a class," Donnelly declared, "I should not support it. It is a declaration that free men will not clothe their limbs in the goods of manufacturers of this slave-making oligarchy. [Loud cheers.] It is war to the knife and the knife to the hilt. [Loud cheers.] I trust that those who have staggered away from this resolution because of the opprobrium that a hireling press has applied to the word boycott, will withdraw their opposition, and that the resolution may be adopted by a rising vote. [Tremendous applause.]" A motion to strike out the boycott clause was overwhelmingly defeated, and the whole resolution was adopted by acclamation.[7]

Among the delegates conspicuous in the uproar was a coal-black Negro, marching about the Coliseum Building with an American flag fluttering from a cane and apparently feeling gaily at home. A number of important Populist leaders not only aimed to unite the discontented of the cities and the countryside. They sought something that no American party has achieved before or since: a political coalition of the poor whites and the poor blacks of the South. The Southern Farmers' Alliance was conspicuously friendly to the Colored Farmers' Alliance. Committees of white Southern Populists ceremoniously met with black colleagues, joint platforms were adopted, and Negro delegates were named to local and national Populist conventions. The most important Southern Populist leader, Tom Watson, of Georgia, regularly held mixed meetings, despite violent attempts to prevent them. "You are kept apart," Watson told his audiences, "that you may be separately fleeced of your earnings. You are made to hate each other because upon that hatred is rested the keystone of the arch of financial despotism which enslaves you both." Often Watson would pledge his white listeners to defend the Constitutional rights of the Negro, asking the whites to take an oath that they would not backslide. When Georgians threatened to lynch a prominent Negro Populist leader, the state witnessed an unprecedented sight. At Watson's call, two thousand white Populists assembled to protect the Negro. For two days and nights, their arms stacked on Watson's veranda, the white men grimly carried out the Populist doctrine that the issue was poverty, not color.[8]

The groups on which Populism was depending for support, so different from the most ardent followers of liberalism, were of-

fered an appropriately different program. The Populists took over the liberal demand for honest, efficient political leaders, but the reformed government was to be no reflection of upper-income, better-educated America. Civil-service reform was not emphasized at Omaha; it smacked too much of establishing a permanent ruling group and contradicted the Jacksonian faith that any well-intentioned American was good enough to carry on government for his fellows.[9] Populist government was to be by and for "the people," or, to use a more revealing phrase that the Populists borrowed from pre-Civil War reformers, by and for "the producers." The Populist reversion to the practice of dividing the population into producers and nonproducers was the surest indication of their view of America. It indicated their belief that "producers"—those who worked with their hands—were the men who really created the wealth of the nation. In the Populist view, the producers should run the country and should receive a value from their labor which gave little or no return to men whose chief function was providing capital.[10]

In their eagerness to increase the political power of the producers, the Populists urged the secret ballot and endorsed three adventurous techniques for direct democracy: the popular election of United States senators; the initiative, giving the voters the right to legislate over the heads of their representatives; and the referendum, providing the voters with a veto over the actions of the legislature. The initiative and referendum proposals seemed so radical in 1892 that their chief advocate at Omaha, a representative of a New Jersey workingmen's organization, had to argue vigorously for including them in the platform, but he was ultimately successful. Populists could not resist any idea that promised to end the political control of corporations.[11] In fact, so intense was the Populist hatred of politics as it was being practiced that the Omaha gathering whooped through a resolution unique in the history of American conventions, conservative or radical. No one who held a federal, state, or municipal office, the delegates decreed, could sit in a future Populist convention.

And all politics or political machinery was but a means; the end was economic and social reform. The Populists swept together the discontent with both Grantism and liberalism into a bold doctrine of continuous state intervention in behalf of the producers. Governments were to stop aiding the corporations, directly or indirectly, and were to start passing legislation beneficial to Americans who had little or no capital. The issue that excited liberals and old-style Republicans so much—the tariff—was just a "sham battle" to the Populists. "We believe," the Omaha platform emphasized, "that the powers of government should be expanded. . .as rapidly and as far as the good sense of an intelligent people and the teachings of experience shall justify, to the end that oppression, injustice and poverty shall eventually cease in the land."

The Populist eye was on the Interstate Commerce Act of 1887, which put controls over railroads, and the Sherman Anti-Trust Act of 1890, which declared combinations in restraint of trade illegal. These the Populists wanted to strengthen and, in the strengthened form, to make the models for state and federal interferences in economic life that would regulate all corporations and would splinter into small units those which had reached the monopoly stage. For years the Populists had watched extremes of wealth piling up, unchecked by legislation; the Omaha platform proposed to reverse, or at least halt, the trend by a graduated federal income tax. In the minds of most Populists, one of the chief enemies of the farmer was a rigid currency system, and the delegates demanded "a national currency, safe, sound and flexible,

issued by the general government only." Government-operated postal savings banks were to take the savings business out of the hands of private bankers. Federal subtreasuries, "or some other system," should be established to loan money to farmers at no more than two percent interest and to see to it that the supply of currency fluctuated with the demand for agricultural credits. "All land now held by railroads and other corporations in excess of their actual needs," the Omaha convention added, ". . .should be reclaimed by the government and held for actual settlers only." On the general subject of the railroads, those prime ogres of the farmers, the Populists were ready for the most drastic kind of governmental power. The United States was to own and operate the railroads. It was, moreover, to own and operate the telegraph and telephone systems, which were approaching the monopoly stage and which the Populists felt were being run with an arrogant disregard of the consumer's interest.

The obvious socialism of these last proposals brought the most anguished of all cries from liberals. They were startled and outraged that free men could seriously propose handing over such great powers to the state, and their vehemence underlined the fundamental difference in the liberal and Populist approaches. The liberal, however much his practices might deviate from his doctrine under the pressure of the corporations, kept his principal emphasis on liberty, the freedom of the individual in political, economic, and social relations, either with another individual or with his government. The Populist did not forget liberty, but in the troubled Nineties, no less than in the confident late Sixties, the essence of liberty to a large number of Americans was the freedom to escape poverty and to rise in economic and social status. The Populists stressed opportunity rather than sheer liberty. Feeling the vise of corporate power and class stratification closing in on them, they were frantically reaching out for any ideological tool that promised to pry back the ominous jaws, whether or not it met the severest tests of freedom.

Most of the Populists, like so many of the liberals, found their hero in Thomas Jefferson. This may have been a tribute to the many-sided Jefferson, but it was also an example of the confusion that results from applying a man's thought in a different age. Liberals looked to the Jefferson who feared centralized power; Populists, to the Jefferson who considered capitalist power the chief enemy of the aspiring masses. Tom Watson, ardent Jeffersonian and bitter opponent of liberalism, caught the heart of Populism when he spoke of the movement's "yearning, upward tendency." Populism's central target, Watson continued, was "monopoly—not monopoly in the narrow sense of the word—but monopoly of power, of place, of privilege, of wealth, of progress." Its battle cry was: "Keep the avenues of honor free. Close no entrance to the poorest, the weakest, the humblest." Re-create an America that said to ambition: "The field is clear, the contest fair; come, and win your share if you can!"[12]

In the elections of 1892 the Populists became the first third party to carry a state since the GOP started on its way in 1856. The contingent of Populist-minded United States Senators rose to five; the number of Representatives to ten. Populist governors were elected in Kansas, North Dakota, and Colorado, while the number of sympathetic state legislators and county officials mounted to fifteen hundred. In the important Illinois election the Democrats swept the state, but the result was more a defeat for the Populist Party than for its doctrines. At the head of the victorious Democratic ticket was John P. Altgeld, who agreed substantially with every important plank in the Omaha platform. As

this burly, tough-minded dissenter led the elegant Inaugural Ball in Chicago, any radical could feel that a new day was swiftly dawning.

The next year the Populists acquired a powerful ally. Hard times settled over the country again, bringing all the jolting effect of a second severe depression in one generation. The twelve months that began in the middle of 1894 have been called the "année terrible" of the post-Civil War period, and the phrase is not overly dramatic for the record of savage strikes and brutal labor repression, deepening agricultural distress, and a national atmosphere of foreboding at the top and bitterness at the bottom.[13]

Never before had the nation seemed so restive. The year 1894 made labor history, with nearly 750,000 workingmen out in militant strikes. The leader of the Pullman strikers, sent to jail by Cleveland's liberalism, sat mulling over the situation and came out a full-blown socialist. "We have been cursed with the reign of gold long enough," Eugene Debs told wildly cheering crowds. ". . .We are on the eve of a universal change."[14] In the clay hills of the South, across the scorched prairies, the farmer's agitation was rapidly becoming, as one supporter described it, "a religious revival, a crusade, a pentecost of politics, in which a tongue of flame sat upon every man."[15] It was "a fanaticism like the crusades," a Kansas observer added. "At night, from ten thousand little white schoolhouse windows, lights twinkled back hope to the stars. . . . They sang. . .with something of the same mad faith that inspired the martyr going to the stake. Far into the night the voices rose, women's voices, children's voices, the voices of old men, of youths and of maidens rose on the ebbing prairie breezes, as the crusaders of the revolution rode home, praising the people's will as though it were God's will and cursing wealth for its iniquity."[16] Hamlin Garland, watching the Populist representatives flail away in Congress, was sure that the country was approaching "a great periodic upheaval similar to that of '61. Everywhere as I went through the aisles of the House, I saw it and heard it. . . . The House is a smoldering volcano."[17]

In Indianapolis, a ruche-collared lady measured the political situation and went off to see the cathedrals of Europe. "I am going to spend my money," she said, "before those crazy people take it."[18]

[1] There is considerable evidence that George was actually counted out. John R. Commons *et al.: History of Labour in the United States* (Macmillan, 1918–35), II, 453; Anna De Mille: *Henry George* (University of North Carolina Press, 1950), p. 152.

[2] E. A. Allen: *The Life and Public Services of James Baird Weaver. . .and. . .of James G. Field. . .[with] an account of the first convention of the People's Party at Omaha* (People's Party Publishing Co., 1892), pp. 91–2.

[3] Ibid., pp. 96–7. The word "touching," an obvious misprint, has been changed to "touches."

[4] Ibid., pp. 100–2; Frank B. Tracy: "Menacing Socialism in the United States," *Forum* (May 1893), XV, 332–4; Mason A. Green: "Edward Bellamy," MS., Harvard University Library, Chap. xv; *Omaha Bee*, July 5–7, 1892.

[5] Godkin, in *Nation* (July 7, 1892), LV, 1; Frederic Bancroft, ed.: *Speeches, Correspondence, and Political Papers of Carl Schurz* (Putnam, 1913), V, 87–121; Elting E. Morison, ed.: *Letters of Theodore Roosevelt* (Harvard University Press, 1951), I, 292.

[6] The platform and supplementary resolution, as printed in Allen, pp. 96–100, 107–11, are used throughout this section.

[7] Ibid, pp. 100–11.

[8] Jack Abramowitz: "The Negro in the Agrarian and Populist Movements," MS., in Mr. Abramowitz's possession; C. Vann Woodward: "Tom Watson and the Negro in Agrarian Politics," *Journal of Southern History* (February 1938), IV, 17–23. The quotation is from ibid., p. 18.

[9] The only mention of civil-service reform in the Omaha platform came in a special instance. In the event of government ownership of the railroads, the Populists wanted "civil service regulation of the most rigid character, so as to prevent the increase of the power of the national administration by the use of such additional government employees." Generally, the Alliance platforms had ignored the merit system, and one Alliance document flatly opposed it with the Jacksonian query: "If this is not the people's government, whose government is it?" (Frank M. Drew, "The Present Farmer's Movement," *Political Science Quarterly* [June 1891], VI, 302). The agrarian leader William Jennings Bryan was to show the same tendency during the campaign of 1896. While conceding the importance of merit appointments, he opposed life tenure because "we do not want to build up an office-holding class." *The First Battle* (W. B. Conkey, Chicago, 1896), p. 460.

[10] Arthur M. Schlesinger, Jr.: *The Age of Jackson* (Little, Brown, 1945), Chap. xxiv, and Destler, pp. 25–9. The Omaha platform pushed the "Producer" doctrine to its logical extreme by declaring: "Wealth belongs to him who creates it, and every dollar taken from industry [i.e., work], without an equivalent, is robbery."

[11] Destler, p. 24, 63 n.

[12] Woodward: *Watson*, p. 217.

[13] The phrase is from Nevins: *Cleveland* (Dodd, Mead, 1947), p. 649. Italics in original.

[14] Ray Ginger: *The Bending Cross, A Biography of Eugene Victor Debs* (Rutgers University Press, 1949), p. 193.

[15] Elizabeth Barr, quoted in John D. Hicks: *The Populist Revolt* (University of Minnesota Press, 1931), p. 159.

[16] William Allen White, quoted in Walter Johnson: *William Allen White's America* (Holt, 1947), p. 54.

[17] Garland: "The Alliance Wedge in Congress," *Arena* (March 1892), V, 455–7.

[18] Interview with the late Charles Beard, who was remembering the remark of a friend of his family.

JOHN D. HICKS (b. 1890), professor emeritus,
University of California, Berkeley, studied at Northwestern
and Wisconsin universities. A native of Missouri, he was
greatly influenced by the American frontier tradition he
knew so well. His provocative study, *The Populist Revolt*,
published in 1931 in the midst of the worst depression in
history, has become a classic. The following selection from
this work presents the standard interpretation of Populism,
which came under attack during the 1950s. Hicks explains
how the Populists made a genuine contribution to the
growth of political and economic democracy.*

John D. Hicks

The Populist Contribution

Early in 1890, when the People's party
was yet in the embryo stage, a farmer editor
from the West set forth the doctrine that "the
cranks always win." As he saw it,

The cranks are those who do not accept the existing order of things, and propose to change them.
The existing order of things is always accepted by
the majority, therefore the cranks are always in the
minority. They are always progressive thinkers
and always in advance of their time, and they
always win. Called fanatics and fools at first, they
are sometimes persecuted and abused. But their
reforms are generally righteous, and time, reason
and argument bring men to their side. Abused and
ridiculed, then tolerated, then respectfully given a
hearing, then supported. This has been the
gauntlet that all great reforms and reformers have
run, from Galileo to John Brown.

The writer of this editorial may have overstated his case, but a backward glance at the
history of Populism shows that many of the
reforms that the Populists demanded, while
despised and rejected for a season, won
triumphantly in the end. The party itself did
not survive, nor did many of its leaders, although the number of contemporary politicians whose escutcheons should bear the bend
sinister of Populism is larger than might be
supposed; but Populistic doctrines showed an
amazing vitality.

* From *The Populist Revolt* by John D. Hicks, copyright 1931 by the University of Minnesota. Pp. 404–423.
Footnotes omitted.

In formulating their principles the Populists reasoned that the ordinary, honest, willing American worker, be he farmer or be he laborer, might expect in this land of opportunity not only the chance to work but also, as the rightful reward of his labor, a fair degree of prosperity. When, in the later eighties and in the "heart-breaking nineties," hundreds of thousands—perhaps millions—of men found themselves either without work to do or, having work, unable to pay their just debts and make a living, the Populists held that there must be "wrong and crime and fraud somewhere." What was more natural than to fix the blame for this situation upon the manufacturers, the railroads, the money-lenders, the middlemen—plutocrats all, whose "colossal fortunes, unprecedented in the history of mankind," grew ever greater while the multitudes came to know the meaning of want. Work was denied when work might well have been given, and "the fruits of the toil of millions were boldly stolen."

And the remedy? In an earlier age the hard-pressed farmers and laborers might have fled to free farms in the seemingly limitless lands of the West, but now the era of free lands had passed. Where, then, might they look for help? Where, if not to the government, which alone had the power to bring the mighty oppressors of the people to bay? So to the government the Populists turned. From it they asked laws to insure a full redress of grievances. As Dr. Turner puts it, "the defences of the pioneer democrat began to shift from free land to legislation, from the ideal of individualism to the ideal of social control through regulation by law." Unfortunately, however, the agencies of government had been permitted to fall into the hands of the plutocrats. Hence, if the necessary corrective legislation were to be obtained, the people must first win control of their government. The Populist philosophy thus boiled down finally to two fundamental propositions; one, that the government must

restrain the selfish tendencies of those who profited at the expense of the poor and needy; the other, that the people, not the plutocrats, must control the government.

In their efforts to remove all restrictions on the power of the people to rule, the Populists accepted as their own a wide range of reforms. They believed, and on this they had frequently enough the evidence of their own eyes, that corruption existed at the ballot box and that a fair count was often denied. They fell in line, therefore, with great enthusiasm when agitators, who were not necessarily Populists, sought to popularize the Australian ballot and such other measures as were calculated to insure a true expression of the will of the people. Believing as they did that the voice of the people was the voice of God, they sought to eliminate indirect elections, especially the election of United States senators by state legislatures and of the president and the vice president by an electoral college. Fully aware of the habits of party bosses in manipulating nominating conventions, the Populists veered more and more in the direction of direct primary elections, urging in some of their later platforms that nominations even for president and vice president should be made by direct vote. Woman suffrage was a delicate question, for it was closely identified with the politically hazardous matter of temperance legislation, but, after all, the idea of votes for women was so clearly in harmony with the Populist doctrine of popular rule that it could not logically be denied a place among genuinely Populistic reforms. Direct legislation through the initiative and referendum and through the easy amendment of state constitutions naturally appealed strongly to the Populists—the more so as they saw legislatures fail repeatedly to enact reform laws to which a majority of their members had been definitely pledged. "A majority of the people," said the Sioux Falls convention, "can never be corruptly influenced." The recall of faithless officials, even judges, also attracted favorable attention from the makers of later Populist platforms.

To list these demands is to cite the chief political innovations made in the United States during recent times. The Australian system of voting, improved registration laws, and other devices for insuring "a free ballot and a fair count" have long since swept the country. Woman suffrage has won an unqualified victory. The election of United States senators by direct vote of the people received the approval of far more than two-thirds of the national House of Representatives as early as 1898; it was further foreshadowed by the adoption, beginning in 1904, of senatorial primaries in a number of states, the results of which were to be regarded as morally binding upon the legislatures concerned; and it became a fact in 1913 with the ratification of the seventeenth amendment to the constitution.

The direct election of president and vice president was a reform hard to reconcile with state control of election machinery and state definition of the right to vote. Hence this reform never made headway; but the danger of one presidential candidate receiving a majority of the popular vote and another a majority of the electoral vote, as was the case in the Cleveland-Harrison contest of 1888, seems definitely to have passed. Recent elections may not prove that the popular voice always speaks intelligently; but they do seem to show that it speaks decisively.

In the widespread use of the primary election for the making of party nominations, the Populist principle of popular rule has scored perhaps its most telling victory. Tillman urged this reform in South Carolina at a very early date, but on obtaining control of the Democratic political machine of his state, he hesitated to give up the power that the convention system placed in his hands. At length, however, in 1896 he allowed the reform to go through. Wisconsin, spurred on by the La Follette forces, adopted the direct primary plan of nominations in 1903, and

thereafter the other states of the Union, with remarkably few exceptions, fell into line. Presidential preference primaries, through which it was hoped that the direct voice of the people could be heard in the making of nominations for president and vice president, were also adopted by a number of states, beginning with Oregon in 1910.

Direct legislation by the people became almost an obsession with the Populists, especially the middle-of-the-road faction, in whose platforms it tended to overshadow nearly every other issue; and it is perhaps significant that the initiative and referendum were first adopted by South Dakota, a state in which the Populist party had shown great strength, as close on the heels of the Populist movement as 1898. Other states soon followed the South Dakota lead, and particularly in Oregon the experiment of popular legislation was given a thorough trial. New constitutions and numerous amendments to old constitutions tended also to introduce much popularly made law, the idea that legislation in a constitution is improper and unwise receiving perhaps its most shattering blow when an Oklahoma convention wrote for that state a constitution of fifty thousand words. The recall of elected officials has been applied chiefly in municipal affairs, but some states also permit its use for state officers and a few allow even judges, traditionally held to be immune from popular reactions, to be subjected to recall. Thus many of the favorite ideas of the Populists, ideas that had once been "abused and ridiculed," were presently "respectfully given a hearing, then supported."

Quite apart from these changes in the American form of government, the Populist propaganda in favor of independent voting did much to undermine the intense party loyalties that had followed in the wake of the Civil War. The time had been when for the Republican voter "to doubt Grant was as bad as to doubt Christ," when the man who scratched his party ticket was regarded as little, if any, better than the traitor to his country. The Alliance in its day had sought earnestly to wean the partisan voter over to independence. It had urged its members to "favor and assist to office such candidates only as are thoroughly identified with our principles and who will insist on such legislation as shall make them effective." And in this regard the Alliance, as some of its leaders boasted, had been a "great educator of the people." The Populist party had to go even further, for its growth depended almost wholly upon its ability to bring voters to a complete renunciation of old party loyalties. Since at one time or another well over a million men cast their ballots for Populist tickets, the loosening of party ties that thus set in was of formidable proportions.

Indeed, the man who became a Populist learned his lesson almost too well. When confronted, as many Populist voters thought themselves to be in 1896, with a choice between loyalty to party and loyalty to principle, the third-party adherent generally tended to stand on principle. Thereafter, as Populism faded out, the men who once had sworn undying devotion to the Omaha platform, were compelled again to transfer their allegiance. Many Republicans became Democrats via the Populist route; many Democrats became Republicans. Most of the Populists probably returned to the parties from which they had withdrawn, but party ties, once broken, were not so strong as they had been before. The rapid passing of voters from one party to another and the wholesale scratching of ballots, so characteristic of voting today, are distinctly reminiscent of Populism; as are also the nonpartisan ballots by which judges, city commissioners, and other officers are now frequently chosen, wholly without regard to their party affiliations.

In the South the Populist demands for popular government produced a peculiar situation. To a very great extent the southern Populists were recruited from the rural classes that had hitherto been politically inarticulate. Through the Populist party the "wool hat boys" from the country sought to obtain the weight in southern politics that their numbers warranted but that the Bourbon dynasties had ever denied them. In the struggle that ensued, both sides made every possible use of the negro vote, and the bugaboo of negro domination was once again raised. Indeed, the experience of North Carolina under a combination government of Populists and Republicans furnished concrete evidence of what might happen should the political power of the negro be restored. Under the circumstances, therefore, there seemed to be nothing else for the white Populists to do but to return to their former allegiance until the menace of the negro voter could be removed.

With the Democratic party again supreme, the problem of negro voting was attacked with right good will. Indeed, as early as 1890 the state of Mississippi, stimulated no doubt by the agitation over the Force Bill, adopted a constitution that fixed as a prerequisite for voting a two years' residence in the state and a one year's residence in the district or town. This provision, together with a poll tax that had to be paid far in advance of the dates set for elections, diminished appreciably the number of negro voters, among whom indigence was common and the migratory propensity well developed. To complete the work of disfranchisement an amendment was added to the Mississippi constitution in 1892 that called for a modified literary test that could be administered in such a way as to permit illiterate whites to vote, while discriminating against illiterate, or even literate, blacks. The Tillmanites in South Carolina found legal means to exclude the negro voter in 1895; Louisiana introduced her famous "grandfather clause" in 1898; North Carolina adopted residence, poll-tax, and educational qualifications in 1900; Alabama followed in 1901; and in their own good time the other southern states in which negro voters had constituted a serious problem did the same thing. Some reverses were experienced in the courts, but the net result of this epidemic of anti-negro suffrage legislation was to eliminate for the time being all danger that negro voters might play an important part in southern politics.

With this problem out of the way, or at least in the process of solution, it became possible for the rural whites of the South to resume the struggle for a voice in public affairs that they had begun in the days of the Alliance and had continued under the banner of Populism. They did not again form a third party, but they did contend freely in the Democratic primaries against the respectable and conservative descendants of the Bourbons. The Tillman machine in South Carolina continued for years to function smoothly as the agency through which the poorer classes sought to dominate the government of that state. It regularly sent Tillman to the United States Senate, where after his death his spirit lived on in the person of Cole Blease. In Georgia the struggle for supremacy between the two factions of the Democratic party was a chronic condition, with now one side and now the other in control. Former Populists, converted by the lapse of time into regular organization Democrats, won high offices and instituted many of the reforms for which they had formerly been derided. Even Tom Watson rose from his political deathbed to show amazing strength in a race for Congress in 1918 and to win an astounding victory two years later when he sought a seat in the United States Senate.

For better or for worse, the political careers of such southern politicians as James K. Vardaman and Theodore G. Bilbo of Mississippi, the Honorable "Jeff." Davis of Arkansas, and Huey P. Long of Louisiana demonstrate conclusively the fact that the lower classes in the South can, and sometimes do, place men of their own kind and choosing in high office. In these later days rural whites, who fought during Populist times with only such support as they could obtain from Republican sources, have sometimes been able to count as allies the mill operatives and their sympathizers in the factory districts; and southern primary elections are now apt to be as exciting as the regular elections are tame. Populism may have had something to do with the withdrawal of political power from the southern negro, but it also paved the way for the political emancipation of the lower class of southern whites.

The control of the government by the people was to the thoughtful Populist merely a means to an end. The next step was to use the power of the government to check the iniquities of the plutocrats. When the Populists at Omaha were baffled by the insistence of the temperance forces, they pointed out that before this or any other such reform could be accomplished they must "ask all men to first help us to determine whether we are to have a republic to administer." The inference is clear. Once permit the people really to rule, once insure that the men in office would not or could not betray the popular will, and such regulative measures as would right the wrongs from which the people suffered would quickly follow. The Populist believed implicitly in the ability of the people to frame and enforce the measures necessary to redeem themselves from the various sorts of oppression that were being visited upon them. They catalogued in their platform the evils from which society suffered and suggested the specific remedies by which these evils were to be overcome.

Much unfair criticism has been leveled at the Populists because of the attitude they took towards the allied subjects of banking and currency. To judge from the contemporary anti-Populist diatribes and from many subsequent criticisms of the Populist financial program, one would think that in such matters the third-party economists were little better than raving maniacs. As a matter of fact, the old-school Populists could think about as straight as their opponents. Their newspapers were well edited, and the arguments therein presented usually held together. Populist literature, moreover, was widely and carefully read by the ordinary third-party voters, particularly by the western farmers, whose periods of enforced leisure gave them ample opportunity for reading and reflection. Old-party debaters did not tackle their Populist antagonists lightly, for as frequently as not the bewhiskered rustic, turned orator, could present in support of his arguments an array of carefully sorted information that left his better-groomed opponent in a daze. The appearance of the somewhat irrelevant silver issue considerably confused Populist thinking, but even so many of the old-timers kept their heads and put silver in its proper place.

The Populists observed with entire accuracy that the currency of the United States was both inadequate and inelastic. They criticized correctly the part played by the national banking system in currency matters as irresponsible and susceptible of manipulation in the interest of the creditor class. They demanded a stabilized dollar, and they believed that it could be obtained if a national currency "safe, sound, and flexible" should be issued direct to the people by the government itself in such quantities as the reasonable demands of business should dictate. Silver and gold might be issued as well as paper, but the value of the dollar should come from the fiat of government and not from the "intrinsic worth" of the metal.

It is interesting to note that since the time when Populists were condemned as lunatics for holding such views legislation has been adopted that, while by no means going the full length of an irredeemable paper currency, does seek to accomplish precisely the ends that the Populists had in mind. Populist and free-silver agitation forced economists to

study the money question as they had never studied it before and ultimately led them to propose remedies that could run the gauntlet of public opinion and of Congress. The Aldrich-Vreeland Act of 1908 authorized an emergency currency of several hundred million dollars, to be lent to banks on approved securities in times of financial disturbance. A National Monetary Commission, created at the same time, reported after four years' intensive study in favor of a return to the Hamiltonian system of a central Bank of the United States. Instead Congress in 1914, under Wilson's leadership, adopted the federal reserve system. The Federal Reserve Act did not, indeed, destroy the national banks and avoid the intervention of bankers in all monetary matters, but it did make possible an adequate and elastic national currency, varying in accordance with the needs of the country, and it placed supreme control of the nation's banking and credit resources in the hands of a federal reserve board, appointed not by the bankers but by the president of the United States with the consent of the Senate. The Populist diagnosis was accepted, and the Populist prescription was not wholly ignored.

Probably no item in the Populist creed received more thorough castigation at the hands of contemporaries than the demand for subtreasuries, or government warehouses for the private storage of grain, but the subtreasury idea was not all bad, and perhaps the Populists would have done well had they pursued it further than they did. The need that the subtreasury was designed to meet was very real. Lack of credit forced the farmer to sell his produce at the time of harvest, when the price was lowest. A cash loan on his crop that would enable him to hold it until prices should rise was all that he asked. Prices might thus be stabilized; profits honestly earned by the farmers would no longer fall to the speculators. That the men who brought forward the subtreasury as a plan for obtaining short-term rural credits also loaded it with an un-workable plan for obtaining a flexible currency was unfortunate; but the fundamental principle of the bill has by no means been discredited. Indeed, the Warehouse Act of 1916 went far towards accomplishing the very thing the Populists demanded. Under it the United States Department of Agriculture was permitted to license warehousemen and authorize them to receive, weigh, and grade farm products, for which they might issue warehouse receipts as collateral. Thus the owner might borrow the money he needed—not, however, from the government of the United States.

In addition to the credits that the subtreasury would provide, Populist platforms usually urged also that the national government lend money on farm lands directly at a low rate of interest. This demand, which received an infinite amount of condemnation and derision at the time, has since been treated with much deference. If the government does not now print paper money to lend the farmer, with his land as security, it nevertheless does stand back of an elaborate system of banks through which he may obtain the credit he needs. Under the terms of the Federal Reserve Act national banks may lend money on farm mortgages—a privilege they did not enjoy in Populist times—and agricultural paper running as long as six months may be rediscounted by the federal reserve banks. From the farm loan banks, created by an act of 1916, the farmers may borrow for long periods sums not exceeding fifty per cent of the value of their land and twenty per cent of the value of their permanent improvements. Finally, through still another series of banks, the federal intermediate credit banks, established by an act of 1923, loans are made available to carry the farmer from one season to the next or a little longer, should occasion demand; the intermediate banks were authorized to rediscount agricultural and livestock paper for periods of from six months to three years. Thus the government has created a comprehensive system of rural credits through which the farmer may obtain either short-term loans, loans of intermediate duration, or long-term loans, as his needs require, with a minimum of difficulty and at minimum interest rates.

It would be idle to indulge in a *post hoc* argument in an attempt to prove that all these developments were due to Populism; but the intensive study of agricultural problems that led ultimately to these measures did begin with the efforts of sound economists to answer the arguments of the Populists. And it is evident that in the end the economists conceded nearly every point for which the Populists had contended.

More recent attempts to solve the agricultural problem, while assuming, as readily as even a Populist could have asked, the responsibility of the government in the matter, have progressed beyond the old Populist panacea of easy credit. Agricultural economists now have their attention fixed upon the surplus as the root of the difficulty. In industry, production can be curtailed to meet the demands of any given time, and a glutted market with the attendant decline in prices can be in a measure forestalled. But in agriculture, where each farmer is a law unto himself and where crop yields must inevitably vary greatly from year to year, control of production is well-nigh impossible and a surplus may easily become chronic. Suggestions for relief therefore looked increasingly towards the disposal of this surplus to the greatest advantage.

The various McNary-Haugen bills that have come before Congress in recent years proposed to create a federal board through which the margin above domestic needs in years of plenty should be purchased and held, or disposed of abroad at whatever price it would bring. Through an "equalization fee" the losses sustained by "dumping" the surplus in this fashion were to be charged back upon the producers benefited. Although this proposition was agreeable to a majority of both houses of Congress, it met opposition from two successive presidents, Coolidge and Hoover, and was finally set aside for another scheme, less "socialistic." In 1929 Congress passed and the president signed a law for the creation of an appointive federal farm board, one of whose duties it is, among others, to encourage the organization of cooperative societies through which the farmers may themselves deal with the problem of the surplus. In case of necessity, however, the board may take the lead in the formation of stabilization corporations, which under its strict supervision may buy up such seasonal or temporary surpluses as threaten to break the market and hold them for higher prices. A huge revolving fund, appropriated by Congress, is made available for this purpose, loans from this fund being obtainable by the stabilization corporations at low interest rates. There is much about this thoroughly respectable and conservative law that recalls the agrarian demands of the nineties. Indeed, the measure goes further in the direction of government recognition of and aid to the principle of agricultural cooperation than even the most erratic Alliancemen could have dared to hope. Perhaps it will prove to be the "better plan" that the farmers called for in vain when the subtreasury was the best idea they could present.

To the middle western Populist the railway problem was as important as any other—perhaps the most important of all. Early Alliance platforms favored drastic governmental control of the various means of communication as the best possible remedy for the ills from which the people suffered, and the first Populist platform to be written called for government ownership and operation only in case "the most rigid, honest, and just national control and supervision" should fail to "remove the abuses now existing." Thereafter the Populists usually demanded government ownership, although it is clear enough from their state and local platforms and from the votes and actions of Populist officeholders that, pending the day when ownership should become a fact, regulation by state and nation must be made ever more effective.

Possibly government ownership is no nearer today than in Populist times, but the first objective of the Populists, "the most rigid, honest, and just national control," is as nearly an accomplished fact as carefully drawn legislation and highly efficient administration can make it. Populist misgivings about governmental control arose from the knowledge that the Interstate Commerce Act of 1887, as well as most regulatory state legislation, was wholly ineffectual during the nineties; but beginning with the Elkins Act of 1903, which struck at the practice of granting rebates, a long series of really workable laws found their way into the statute books. The Hepburn Act of 1906, the Mann-Elkins Act of 1910, and the Transportation Act of 1920, not to mention lesser laws, placed the Interstate Commerce Commission upon a high pinnacle of power. State laws, keeping abreast of the national program, supplemented national control with state control; and through one or the other agency most of the specific grievances of which the Populists had complained were removed. The arbitrary fixing of rates by the carriers, a commonplace in Populist times, is virtually unknown today. If discriminations still exist between persons or places, the Interstate Commerce Commission is apt to be as much to blame as the railroads. Free passes, so numerous in Populist times as to occasion the remark that the only people who did not have passes were those who could not afford to pay their own fare, have virtually ceased to be issued except to railway employes. Railway control of state governments, even in the old Granger states, where in earlier days party bosses took their orders directly from railway officials, has long since become a thing of the past. The railroads still may have an influence in politics, but the railroads do not rule. Governmental control of telephones, telegraphs, and pipe lines, together with such later developments as the radio and the transmission of electric power, is accepted today as a matter of course, the issues being merely to what extent control should go and through what agencies it should be accomplished.

For the trust problem, as distinguished from the railroad problem, the Populists had no very definite solution. They agreed, however, that the power of government, state and national, should be used in such a way as to prevent "individuals or corporations fastening themselves, like vampires, on the people and sucking their substance." Antitrust laws received the earnest approval of Alliancemen and Populists and were often initiated by them. The failure of such laws to secure results was laid mainly at the door of the courts, and when Theodore Roosevelt in 1904 succeeded in securing an order from the United States Supreme Court dissolving the Northern Securities Company, it was hailed as a great victory for Populist principles. Many other incidental victories were won. Postal savings banks "for the safe deposit of the earnings of the people" encroached upon the special privileges of the bankers. An amendment to the national constitution in 1913, authorizing income taxes, recalled a contrary decision of the Supreme Court, which the Populists in their day had cited as the best evidence of the control of the government by the trusts; and income and inheritance taxes have ever since been levied. The reform of state and local taxation so as to exact a greater proportion of the taxes from the trusts and those who profit from them has also been freely undertaken. Labor demands, such as the right of labor to organize, the eight-hour day, limitation of injunctions in labor disputes, and restrictions on im-

migration were strongly championed by the Populists as fit measures for curbing the power of the trusts and were presently treated with great consideration. The Clayton Antitrust Act and the Federal Trade Commission Act, passed during the Wilson regime, were the products of long experience with the trust problem. The manner in which these laws have been enforced, however, would seem to indicate that the destruction of the trusts, a common demand in Populist times, is no longer regarded as feasible and that by government control the interests of the people can best be conserved.

On the land question the Populist demands distinctly foreshadowed conservation. "The land," according to the Omaha declaration, "including all the natural resources of wealth, is the heritage of all the people and should not be monopolized for speculative purposes." Land and resources already given away were of course difficult to get back, and the passing of the era of free lands could not be repealed by law, but President Roosevelt soon began to secure results in the way of the reclamation and irrigation of arid western lands, the enlargement and protection of the national forests, the improvement of internal waterways, and the withdrawal from entry of lands bearing mineral wealth such as coal, oil, and phosphates. At regular intervals, since 1908, the governors of the states have met together in conference to discuss the conservation problem, and this once dangerous Populist doctrine has now won all but universal acceptance.

It would thus appear that much of the Populist program has found favor in the eyes of later generations. Populist plans for altering the machinery of government have, with but few exceptions, been carried into effect. Referring to these belated victories of the Populists, William Allen White, the man who had once asked, "What's the matter with Kansas?" wrote recently, "They abolished the established order completely and ushered in a new order." Mrs. Mary E. Lease looked back proudly in 1914 on her political career:

In these later years I have seen, with gratification, that my work in the good old Populist days was not in vain. The Progressive party has adopted our platform, clause by clause, plank by plank. Note the list of reforms which we advocated which are coming into reality. Direct election of senators is assured. Public utilities are gradually being removed from the hands of the few and placed under the control of the people who use them. Woman suffrage is now almost a national issue. . . . The seed we sowed out in Kansas did not fall on barren ground.

Thanks to this triumph of Populist principles, one may almost say that, in so far as political devices can insure it, the people now rule. Political dishonesty has not altogether disappeared and the people may yet be betrayed by the men they elect to office, but on the whole the acts of government have come to reflect fairly clearly the will of the people. Efforts to assert this newly won power in such a way as to crush the economic supremacy of the predatory few have also been numerous and not wholly unsuccessful. The gigantic corporations of today, dwarfing into insignificance the trusts of yesterday, are, in spite of their size, far more circumspect in their conduct than their predecessors. If in the last analysis "big business" controls, it is because it has public opinion on its side and not merely the party bosses.

To radicals of today, however, the Populist panaceas, based as they were upon an essentially individualistic philosophy and designed merely to insure for every man his right to "get ahead" in the world, seem totally inadequate. These latter-day extremists point to the perennial reappearance of such problems as farm relief, unemployment, unfair taxation, and law evasion as evidence that the Populist type of reform is futile, that something more drastic is required. Nor is their contention without point. It is reasonable to suppose that progressivism itself must progress; that the programs that would provide solutions for the problems of one generation might fall far short of meeting the needs of a succeeding generation. Perhaps one may not agree with the view of some present-day radicals that only a revolution will suffice and that the very attempt to make existing institutions more tolerable is treason to any real progress, since by so doing the day of revolution is postponed; but one must recognize that when the old Populist panaceas can receive the enthusiastic support of Hooverian Republicans and Alsmithian Democrats these once startling demands are no longer radical at all. One is reminded of the dilemma that Alice of Wonderland encountered when she went through the looking-glass into the garden of live flowers. On and on she ran with the Red Queen, but however fast they went they never seemed to pass anything.

"Well, in our country," said Alice, still panting a little, "you'd generally get to somewhere else—if you ran very fast for a long time as we've been doing."

"A slow sort of country!" said the Queen. "Now here, you see, it takes all the running you can do to keep in the same place. If you want to get somewhere else, you must run twice as fast as that!"

The growing interest during the depressed 1930s in the roots of progressive political thought yielded, among other studies, *The People's Party in Texas*, a penetrating analysis of the movement in one state. The author, ROSCOE C. MARTIN (b. 1903), is a professor of government and a specialist in public administration. He has written extensively on local, state, and federal problems. In this selection he presents an incisive explanation of the causes of the rise of Populism in Texas and the difficulties it faced as a third party. He focuses attention also on influences other than those of the frontier and on the contributions that the Populists made to the politics of the state. *

Roscoe C. Martin

The Texas Experience

It is necessary to note, by way of background, that Texas in 1890 presented certain features which must be borne in mind when this State is considered as a field of action for political parties. First, it was a one-party state, with the Democratic Party in a position of dominance; second, it was essentially an agricultural empire. Its preference for Democracy and its agrarian nature must be grasped by one who would understand any important phase of local politics during the last decade of the nineteenth century.

A further consideration of importance grows from the grievances nursed by the farmer from the time of the Civil War on. First, there were certain conditions in the field of politics which were not to his liking. Again, there were many phases of the agricultural problem which demanded adjustment, as for example those pertaining to prices obtained for farm products and to the marketing system. Further, in the field of transportation conditions were equally unsatisfactory. The railroads, of course, were the chief object of the citizen's wrath, or solicitude, in this direction. Finally, there was much that might be subjected to criticism in the domain of public finance: in the sphere of the Federal Government, it was apparent (to the farmer) there was too little money, while in that of the State the system of taxation seemed unfair and unjust.

* Roscoe C. Martin, *The People's Party in Texas* (Austin: University of Texas Press, 1933), pp. 252–268. Reprinted by permission of The University of Texas and the Bureau of Research in the Social Sciences. Most footnotes omitted.

Thus dissatisfied, it is not strange that the farmer sought relief by organization during the last quarter of the century. The Grange, the first nation-wide post-War movement among the farmers, early revealed serious shortcomings, and its place, in a sense, soon was taken by the Greenback Party, which came to the front for a brief period to advocate politically the financial views of the farmer. Followed the Farmers' Alliance, which in turn gave way to the People's Party, as had the Grange to the Greenback Party. The Grange, the Greenback Party, and the Alliance, all strong in Texas in their day, served to flat-break the ground for Populism, which followed in due time.

When Governor Hogg assumed office in 1890, he found himself in a most difficult position. The discontented elements, temporarily quieted by the new Governor's vigorous championship of the railroad commission, soon became active again; and ere long their leaders and the Governor were again at loggerheads. Eventually an issue was named on which battle was joined. It was found in the subtreasury plan of the Alliance, which, espoused by the malcontents, was rejected by the Governor and his party advisers. Cut to the quick by the action of the Democratic spokesmen, which virtually ostracized them from that party, the subtreasury men segregated themselves in a group called the "subtreasury" or "Jeffersonian" Democrats. Meanwhile a new political party, the People's Party, had come into being. Some investigation revealed that the new party and the Alliance were not greatly different in the important respects of leadership and program. There seemed, then, little reason for maintaining separate organizations for Jeffersonians and Populists, and the two groups fused, in April, 1892, to form the People's Party of Texas.

The program of the new party offered little that was new. Resting basically in the old Jeffersonian idea that all men were created free and equal, it insisted on adjustments in the fields of land, which under its theory ought to be preserved against the large and more especially the alien landholders; transportation, in which domain the railroads demanded strict regulation; and money, of which, as every Populist knew, there was too little in circulation. To these major demands were added some, as for example those relating to tax reform and trust regulation, of an auxiliary though important nature. Of a piece with the demand for fiat equality in the world of economics were the suggestions in the field of politics for the popular election of officers, short terms, limitations on re-elections, low salaries for public officials, direct legislation and the recall, and proportional representation. All or virtually all of these proposals grew logically from Populist adherence to the theory that all men are equal in rights and that the government therefore must guarantee them substantial economic equality and grant them equality in public rights and privileges.

Socially and economically, the new party depended largely on the support of the poor, small farmer for its voting strength, which fact stamped it as preponderantly a rural party. Its vote among the farmers was greatly increased by the support of the Farmers' Alliance, which came over into the Populist camp bag and baggage in the early days of the party. In addition to the poor farmers, the People's Party drew on the sheep ranchmen for support, and upon workingmen in general. Among merchants and professional classes it was all but ignored.

In the field of politics, the Third Party grew historically out of the old Greenback movement whose chief dogmas it accepted as its own. Its adherents, nevertheless, were whilom Democrats for the greater part. Now and then the Republicans came to its assistance, and throughout the decade the Socialists and the Prohibitionists supported its candidates with a large percentage of their voting strength. The party therefore drew on divers sources in the world of politics, though it was regarded rightly as a malcontent organization comprising chiefly renegade Democrats.

The People's Party was, however, something more than an ordinary political party, for it partook strongly of the nature of a religious order. Its leaders were for the most part staunch believers, as were the rank and file, and the Bible was referred to frequently as the final authority for the Populist creed. The Reformers were Protestants almost to a man, and their zeal made it easy enough for their political adversaries to stigmatize them as anti-Catholics, though apparently there was little justice in the charge.

In the matter of racial distribution, the People's Party drew largely upon whites who were native-born of native-born parentage, who comprised some 63 per cent of the State's total population. In the colored districts, whose population equalled 22 per cent of the State's total, the Third Party was forced usually to yield to the Democratic Party and frequently also to the Republican. Among the "foreign" population (i.e., the population either foreign-born or native-born of foreign-born parents), which comprised 15 per cent of the State's total population, the party made few converts. In the Mexican counties of South Texas the strength of Populism was negligible, as it was also in the German districts of Central Texas. Among the minor racial groups, the Czechs, the Poles, and the Swedes, the Reform Party likewise was almost wholly impotent. Hence it may be concluded that it was very largely a party of white, 100 per cent natives, with some little support among the negroes but none of consequence among the so-called foreign elements.

As regards the important element of leadership, the Third Party appeared at first blush to be well fortified. Particularly in the field of state leadership did its position seem strong, for it boasted the adherence of leaders who symbolized the Populist myth of justness and honor, who were very effective as speakers, and who possessed considerable ability as organizers. Some reflection will reveal, however, that the state leaders were not as strong in every respect as they at first appeared, for by important standards by which the qualities of political leadership may be judged they betrayed certain grave if not fatal weaknesses. In the domain of local politics, the party of Reform profited in certain counties from the allegiance of some very able leaders whose significance to Populism is demonstrable. In most sections, however, the Democratic Party maintained a distinct superiority in leadership at the lower level, and the conclusion is warranted that the Third Party, not overly strong in state leadership, was much weaker in the county.

In organization the People's Party, springing as it did from the Farmers' Alliance, profited directly from the machinery of the parent order. On its own account, it devised an hierarchy of primaries and conventions which paralleled the Alliance scheme rather closely. Like its progenitor, the Third Party boasted active units called Populist clubs which were found by the thousands during the heyday of Populism. . . .

The propaganda techniques of the People's Party may be divided into two classes. First there were the methods employed for converting non-believers and strengthening the spirit of the faithful in times of peace. Among those methods was the educational campaign, pursued unceasingly through the agencies of printed appeals and Reform speakers. Ably abetting the educational campaign was a type of appeal which took into account the emotional weaknesses of the people. A brilliant summation of the Populist peace time propaganda methods was found in the camp-meeting, an adaptation of the old religious festival known familiarly by the same name, where educational and emotional appeals were combined into a powerful weapon for Populism.

A second and frequently entirely different type of technique was that found in connection with the campaign proper. Here the leaders of the party appointed a state campaign committee or a campaign manager, under whose direction a vigorous battle, both in words and in writing, was waged with the opposing forces. Hand in hand with the campaign waged throughout the State were the battles fought at the level of the county under the direction of the local Populist chieftains. By far the most interesting phases of the local campaign were to be seen in those sections where some degree of bossism developed, as in the negro districts of Central and East Texas. There the Populist manager was forced frequently to resort to direct action, barter with the negro "'fluence men," and organize "owl meetings" after the fashion of the times. The campaign which resulted, both state and local, often was bitter and acrimonious in the extreme. The Democrats stood their ground, and feelings were aroused which long out-lived the campaign which gave them birth.

Properly considered along with the subject of Populist propaganda and campaign techniques is the Reform press which played an important part in both peace time and election campaigns. The leaders of the Third Party from the first encouraged the growth of Reform journals, and the weekly *Advance* and later the weekly *Mercury*, which served the party in turn as state organs, were established in response to their demand. Populist weeklies also were set up throughout most of the State to the number, at the height of Populism, of about 100. Reform newspapers operated under severe limitations but were able nevertheless, through the medium of editorials, articles by loyal authors, letters from sympathizers, poems, and cartoons, to perform valuable services for the party. Their vigor and enthusiasm, however, were more than offset by their lack of numerical strength, for as compared with the Democratic press that of the People's Party was very weak.

The equipment and techniques thus far considered brought to the Third Party only a modicum of success at the polls. In state elections the executive offices remained free from Populist encroachments, though a few Reform candidates were elected to the Legislature. There they introduced, spoke for, and voted almost unanimously for bills designed to carry into effect the demands of their party. Since the Democratic majority refused to listen to their suggestions, few bills sponsored by them were passed, though they were able to make their presence felt by combining with the retrenchment Democrats. . . .

It was too much to expect that the Democratic Party would submit to the indignities heaped upon it by the advocates of Populism without rising to the defense of its name, its platform, and its spokesmen. In the beginning, it is true, the managers of the old party, being engaged in domestic housecleaning, were inclined to ignore the People's Party. In time, however, they recognized the seriousness of the situation and evolved a defense more than adequate to withstand the charges of their adversaries. Employing all the strategy at their command, and resorting to "strong arm" tactics when the occasion demanded, they literally overwhelmed the Populists in a merciless counter-campaign. The party of Reform, evincing surprising stamina, approached its third campaign with considerable confidence. Meanwhile, however, darkening clouds were gathering on the horizon. The free silver agitation had reached such proportions that the national Democracy was constrained to espouse the cause of the white metal, and with its decision was sounded the death knell of Populism. Numerous factors contributed to the decline of the People's Party, which, active and robust in 1896, had lost all semblance of its former strength by the end of the century.

It is in order now to offer certain observations concerning the People's Party and the study here made of it. The nature of these observations may be indicated by a number of questions, a discussion of which will bring out the points which appear to deserve emphasis. First, in what terms may the rise of the People's Party be explained? Second, what are the obstacles which confront a minor party, and how did these difficulties operate on the Third Party in Texas? Third, what are the services which a minor party may be expected to perform? In what manner did the People's Party, particularly in this State, execute the functions which might legitimately have been expected of it? . . .

Of the various acceptable explanations of the phenomenon called Populism none is more attractive than that which characterizes the movement as a child of the Frontier. The late Professor Frederick Jackson Turner has pointed out how the staunch individualism of the pioneer shades off gradually into a demand for protection and assistance by the government; how the rugged equality originally enforced by the conditions of frontier life thus becomes a legal equality guaranteed by law; and how the changed attitude is evidenced by agitation for free silver and greenback money, trust regulation, popular election and short terms for all officials, direct legislation and the recall, and other dogmas too numerous to record. This authority indeed has gone further: he has analyzed the ideology of Populism and has so correlated it with the geographical distribution of Populist strength as to leave little doubt of the fundamental correctness of his conclusions. Nor do they suffer when applied to the People's Party in Texas. There is much to be said for the proposition that this State in the nineties was yet frontier territory. Without pressing that point, there is no question but that its western and west-central portions were in the frontier stage of development. And, supporting Professor Turner's thesis, it was precisely in the west-central counties that Populism had its greatest vogue in Texas. It was those counties which furnished the staunchest leaders of the Third Party; it was there that men talked most about equality, that they revolted first,

fought hardest, and surrendered last. The Populist movement, in Texas and elsewhere, was a complex of many forces, not least among which were the conditions and the state of mind bred of frontier life.

A second explanation of the People's Party (which in no way conflicts with the first) takes into account sectional interests. . . . From this point of view, a party consists of those who, from their interests, cannot afford not to co-operate, who expect to receive some direct benefit from their adherence to the cause. A new party therefore arises when shifting interests demand a partial or complete realignment of loyalties. Thus the People's Party becomes a mouthpiece for the farmers of the Mid-West, the silver men of the Mountain area, and the farmers of the South, who combine on a program of manifold demands, chief and most potent among which is that for free silver. It requires no great erudition to see what is the value of this explanation of the national parties, nor is its merit appreciably diminished when applied to the State. It is clear at once that the People's Party in Texas existed chiefly to give voice to the demands of the impoverished farmers and that, while its leaders locally made an earnest effort to command the support of other interest groups, it remained largely an agency through which the agrarians made known their desires.

A third thesis of demonstrable validity recognizes that there are times when the old parties are content to wage sham battles over traditional issues, so that interests which require attention must command a new champion. To illustrate, the national major parties in 1890 had grown fat and lazy in their contests over issues of twenty years' standing, and in 1912 they again were coming rapidly to a similar point of sterility. In the first instance, the People's Party rose to put an end to the knightly tournaments of the traditional combatants; in the second, the Progressive movement injected a new vigor into national politics. Minor parties come to the front, then, when political campaigns degenerate into a species of shadow boxing. In these terms may be explained in part the rise of the People's Party in Texas. In 1890, the Democratic Party of Texas had not had its mettle tested seriously in fifteen years. Consequently its helmsmen had learned to steer a serene middle course which encouraged, nay made necessary, the defection of those who desired action. Hence the People's Party came into being in part because of the refusal of the dominant party to deal with the issues of the day.

A final explanation of Populism rests on the idea that on occasion the leaders of the old party or parties will become so tyrannical in their actions as to foment rebellion in the ranks. The idea doubtless is somewhat far-fetched as a plausible explanation of the rise of new national parties, though local situations which might give rise to revolt can readily be imagined. In Texas in 1890 such a situation existed. It appeared, for example, that a definite line of succession to the Governorship had been established, with the Attorney General advancing as a matter of right to the higher office after the traditional two terms of service. Further, there was considerable dissatisfaction at the domination of the Democratic Party by the "Tyler Gang." The Governor, James Stephen Hogg, was from Tyler (in Smith County); the Chairman of the State Executive Committee, N. W. Finley, was from Tyler; and when in 1891 the Governor appointed to fill a vacancy in the United States Senate his life-long friend and associate, Horace Chilton, of Tyler, it was almost too much for the voter to bear. Murmurings of discontent swelled rapidly into a chorus of charges of boss rule, and the People's Party of Texas sprang to the defense of the voter against the alleged clique.

The Third Party in Texas therefore may be understood only in the light of consideration of various forces. If it was in part a movement growing from the frontier spirit of equality translated into a demand for government protection and aid, it was also, and quite logically, a movement which rested on sectional social and economic interests; if it sprang in part from the refusal of the major parties (or, in Texas, the major party) to deal with significant issues, it was likewise in some sense a rebellion against the tyranny of the Democratic leaders. It was, then, of manifold sources and motives.

A minor party, whatever its character, labors under certain handicaps which obstruct its road to success. It must, if it wishes to maintain itself as a semi-permanent force in politics, hold out to its supporters some tangible hope of capturing the government offices at the level at which it seeks to operate; it must, in brief, promise to become a major party in order to establish itself as a serious threat to the existing parties. Notwithstanding the positive need, or at any rate the acknowledged utility, of a definite hope for success at the polls, it is an extremely difficult task for third party leaders to achieve any considerable electoral successes. . . .

To begin with, the new party which aspires to national prominence finds that many accepted practices in politics, some constitutional or legal and others customary, block its path. . . .

A second difficulty faced by minor parties relates with equal weight to state and national politics. It pertains to the drafting of a program which will be acceptable to all dissident elements. The problem is intensified by the fact that the more congenial factions presumably are arrayed already into the opposing camps of the major parties, so that the third party leader is confronted with the task of adjusting the differences of mutually antagonistic and frequently irreconcilable elements whose only bond oftentimes is their discontent. The difficulty of reconciling these malcontents, apparent in the case of the national People's Party, may be seen also in that of the Third Party of Texas. Here there were disillusioned Democrats, Republicans, Greenbackers, Socialists, and Prohibitionists who demanded to be recognized in the party's program, and "post-oak" Americans, Negroes, Germans, Mexicans, and other racial groups which ought likewise to be recognized. Along with the consideration of the diversity of available materials from which a minor party may be coined goes the factor of sectionalism. It may be, as has been said, that sectionalism is hateful to the American mind, but this does not obviate the fact that parties are and seemingly must be based upon sectional interests. It is, however, a matter of extreme difficulty for a minor party to put together enough strength in various sections of the country to carry the day nationally. Locally also the appeal to special interests frequently goes awry. Thus in Texas the Populist appeal to the native white American farmer was very strong, so strong indeed that it served in part to alienate other social and economic and racial groups that might otherwise have professed Populism. The minor party then has a delicate course to steer, for it must at once appeal to and beware of special interests and localism; and by its ability properly to balance its policy regarding these factors is determined in part, and perhaps in large part, its success.

A third handicap confronting minor parties, both nationally and locally, arises from the need for and the difficulty of procuring adequate financial backing. Money almost always comes slowly into the coffers of the third party, for strong financial interests usually are too firmly entrenched in the existing parties to deem it advantageous to contribute to the chest of a new and untried organization. . . .

Again, new parties often take the field under leaders who lack both reputation and experience in politics. The Popocrats of 1896, it is true, found an inspiring leader in the person of Bryan, while the Progressives in 1912 commanded the services of the talismanic Roosevelt. The People's Party as such, however, numbered among its leaders no such prophets but was forced to rely on lesser lights for guidance. In Texas the party won the adherence of some prominent men of personal repute and ability, among them a few of political experience, but the foremost politicians of the State eschewed Populism as it were a plague. The truth is, political leaders are thoroughly familiar with the dangers of revolt. Further, they "know the ropes" under the existing setup; and if at any particular time they do not occupy places of influence, they entertain the eternal hope that things will take a turn for the better and they will be placed in power. They are concerned, then, with the maintenance of the existing alignment; they turn a deaf ear to the importunities of reformers. Minor parties therefore are forced to look among the less skilled, the less heroic, and mayhap the less able for their leaders. It was so of the national People's Party, and it was no less so of the People's Party of Texas.

A different sort of obstacle has been found by some authorities of eminence in the character of the American people. The voters of this country, it has been said, are very fond of association and very sensitive to charges of disloyalty. Further, they have a considerable faith in and regard for order and the established authority, with the net result that they have become a well disciplined army. Nor are they content to pursue their manifold ways in peace: the orthodoxy of the Puritans has transferred itself from the church into other fields, carrying with it unreasoning loyalty to institutions long established and contempt for and fear of those of recent origin or those beyond the pale.

In politics this state of mind has made for a traditionalism which has been the wonder of foreign observers and the subject of caustic comment by American writers. The party provides a place of refuge for those who need social and group intercourse; its dogmas come to be accepted as revealed gospel; a creed of conformity envelops the voter, demanding above all things party loyalty and regularity. Party fetishism thus takes the place of volitional action until in many quarters if not in most the voter has no option but to "vote the ticket": as Brand Whitlock has put it, adherence to one party or the other becomes a matter, not of intellectual choice, but of biological selection. Once this attitude has been created, the notorious inertia of the electorate takes care of the matter of consistency and continuity. Bryce has recognized something of that inertia in a telling phrase, "The Fatalism of the Multitude," which characterizes it in a manner which cannot be here improved.

The significance of the above-described attitude for the student of minor parties should be at once and compellingly apparent. With special reference to the People's Party in Texas, it may be recalled in briefest fashion that Texas in 1890 was traditionally a one-party state; that the Republican Party had been of little consequence and less repute since Reconstruction, sharing with the negro, in the popular mind, the odium for having brought the State to the verge of chaos; and that the Democratic Party had risen as the saviour of Texas, bearing that title with such grace that its position as "the party" had become impregnable. Whole counties there were which boasted not a single white Republican. The people, overwhelmingly Democratic in their sympathies, were of no mind to be converted to heresies.[1]

Minor parties, then, encounter innumerable obstacles in their march toward

---

[1] It is worthy of observation here that the Populist party suffered for some of the sins of its forbears and its contemporaries in minor party politics. Greenbackism, Union Laborism, Prohibitionism, and like panaceas had made the voter wary of third party "isms" and had rendered it necessary for a minor party to prove first of all that it was not harebrained.

success, and the wonder is, not that so many have failed, but that so many have succeeded, in the common acceptance of the word succeed. If the national People's Party was heir to all the ills of minor party politics, the Third Party of Texas found its path likewise beset by what proved to be insuperable difficulties. The Populists, in sum, fought valiantly, but the odds against them were too great.

The People's Party therefore failed most miserably, if as the criterion of success one accepts the idea that the purpose of a political party is to gain control of the government by electing its candidates to office. Indeed, in this sense, if our national history points the way, a minor party may expect to succeed wholly and so become a major party, as did the Republican Party, or to fail completely and pass off the scene, as have most minor parties; for apparently there is no place in our system for a permanent or semi-permanent third party. But if our history records the failure in one sense of the People's Party, it also suggests a different yardstick for the calculation of the successes of minor parties, a yardstick which by comparison makes the first criterion seem rather crude. Third parties, it has been pointed out repeatedly, ordinarily are parties of principle, and their very existence serves usually to indicate the presence of issues either ignored or avoided by the old parties. A more just criterion for judging of the success and worth of a third party may, therefore, be found in the answer to the question, what were the effects of the party upon political issues and the tone of public life?

Judged by this criterion, the People's Party presents an entirely different aspect. In the field of national politics, it forced the Democratic Party to the drastic step of accepting its cardinal demand and nominating Bryan on a free silver platform. Thus it virtually recast that party, causing it to renounce the leadership of Cleveland and become, in effect, a new party whose nature is revealed by the appellation, "the Popocratic party," with which it was endowed by the gold standard men. In Texas the Democrats early began the process of absorption of Reform principles which has not ended to the present day. In 1894 they wrote into their platform the Populist demand regarding convict labor; in 1896 they approved the national Populist planks calling for free silver, the non-retirement of legal tender notes, the abolition of the national banks as banks of issue, the election of United States Senators by popular vote, and the income tax, and the state planks demanding a reform in the fee system and a mechanics' and laborers' lien law; in 1898 they appropriated the Third Party protest against the indiscriminate issuance by the railroads of free passes. In view of the fact that a railroad commission amendment and an alien land law had been carried earlier, the seizure of these planks by the Democrats left the Populists few issues regarded by them as vital. They had succeeded, then, beyond their wildest dreams, for in an important sense they had converted the Democratic Party to Populism.

But the services of the People's Party did not end with the championship of new issues. The old parties, state and national, in 1890 had allowed their zest of youth to degenerate into the complacency of middle age, their ideals into the familiar party traditions. Politics thus had become a workaday business, with little to disturb its serenity. It remained for the People's Party, bursting rudely in upon the placid scene, to revivify our political life by its espousal of principles once known but long forgotten by the major parties. "Restore the government to the people!" was the cry which resounded from the lips of Populists the country over, whether fusionists of Nebraska or mid-roaders of Texas, and its echo came back with redoubled volume years later from the lips of Roosevelt's Progressives.

The spirit of idealism implicit in Populism, if somewhat removed from the realm of achievement, was genuine; its value, if intangible, was real.

The Third Party therefore may be said to have discharged satisfactorily the functions incumbent upon it as a minor party and thus to have achieved a large measure of success. In résumé, it may be noted, with particular reference to the People's Party of Texas, that it liberalized public thought and sentiment, making it safe if not popular to voice one's honest opinions on the issues of the day; it served, through its speakers and its press, as an educator of the populace of no mean influence; it struck lusty blows at, though it was not able to change markedly, the state of mind separating the South from the North; it kept up a steady bombardment against extravagance and profligacy in public expenditures and against corruption in public office, thereby participating in the (supposed) mitigation of those evils: and, most importantly, it brought forward issues which long had been side-stepped or ignored by the dominant party and urged them to such purpose that that party was forced to take action, frequently along the lines recommended by the Populists, in self-defense. The action taken had the ultimate effect of despatching the Third Party, which thus gave its very life to the cause in whose behalf it had been conceived, the victim of its own effectiveness.

In conclusion, attention may be called again to the necessity for bearing in mind the relation between the People's Party of Texas and the national People's Party. The Third Party in this State was not an entity in itself, but an integral part of the national organization, as is evidenced by the collapse of the local movement along with the national with the appropriation by the Democrats of the free silver issue.

Among the first scholars to emphasize the middle-class appeal of Populism was DAVID SAPOSS (b. 1886), a well-known economist and sociologist who applied the techniques of the interdisciplinarian. A native of Russia, a student at Wisconsin and Columbia Universities, and author of various studies including *Left Wing Unionism* (1926), *The Labor Movement in Post-war France* (1931), and *Communism in American Unions* (1959), he wrote the following essay in 1935, when scholars became concerned with middle-class movements. Like others, he worried lest segments of American liberalism be diverted to a fascist course. Some penetrating observations about the future of Populist thought anticipate the arguments of critics of the 1950s.*

David Saposs

Development of Populism in the United States

Events in the United States have dictated a course somewhat different from that followed by the populists of European and other countries. The Granger movement, and its successor, the populist movement, supported a program similar to that of their confreres in other countries, even demanding the ownership of natural monopolies and organizing into separate political parties. After the Spanish-American War, when capitalism emerged as the dominant molder of our culture and the chief source of control of our government, the populist elements, under the guidance of Bryan, and later Wilson, adopted the capitalist conception of "rugged individualism." La Follette and the Progressive Republicans took a somewhat similar position. They began to favor negative legislation that would hold capitalism in check, but shied from positive legislation that would aid the "sufferers" of capitalism.

In assuming this attitude they were considerably influenced by the corruption in our state and municipal governments, as revealed by the then so-called "muckrakers." The capitalistic interests, on the other hand, took advantage of this "horror" of the public in order to discredit government in general. And the populists credulously became the victims of the hoax. Organized labor, under the aegis of Samuel Gompers, as an ally of the populists, also accepted "rugged individualism" by

* From David Saposs, "The Role of the Middle Class in Social Development," in Horace Taylor (ed.), *Economic Essays in Honor of Wesley Clair Mitchell* (New York: Columbia University Press, 1935), pp. 402–413.

warning the workers to avoid becoming "wards of the state." The populists thus abandoned their demand for government ownership and contented themselves with demanding regulation. The prosperity, surcharged with patriotism, that followed the Spanish-American War also tended to divert interest from social questions so that populism disintegrated organizationally, scattering into such localized groups as the La Follette and Bryan elements and lesser groups in the South and Far West. In contrast to its counterpart in Europe, the middle class ceased to be a powerfully organized force.

But since the depression set in, there have been definite indications in this country of the world-wide revival of the middle class. The drift in the elections of the fall of 1932 and the spring of 1933 was definitely away from the party in control. The Democrats replaced the Republicans in many localities and even came into control of the House of Representatives. The assertiveness of the middle-class elements was rather inarticulate and haphazard. It manifested itself by the revolt of the House of Representatives, under the leadership of LaGuardia, against the sales tax and President Hoover's economy program, which measures they contended were designed to aid big business at the expense of the small man. Such a seasoned politician as Governor Roosevelt sensed this undercurrent of discontent and in his presidential campaign championed the interests of the "forgotten man" as against those of Wall Street. Senator Huey Long of Louisiana and Governor Murray of Oklahoma, attempted to reorganize the shattered forces of southern and western populism. The La Follette–Norris group began tightening the lines of their forces in the Northwest. The more desperate and destitute elements were being corralled by the Jobless Party and Father Cox's Hunger Marchers, as well as by the Bonus Expeditionary Forces and their offspring the "Khaki Shirts." The American Legion and other mass organizations have also been struck by this middle-class lightning. Even the professional and intellectual populist elements have organized themselves into the League for Independent Political Action under the leadership of Professor John Dewey.

Organized labor is likewise bestirring itself. In the past periods of unrest it has aligned itself primarily with the populist elements. This has been the case from the very inception of the American labor movement, and the practice has continued up to the present. In the 1890's the Knights of Labor joined in forming the People's Party. Later the American Federation of Labor supported Bryan. More recently it supported Wilson, and as late as 1924 it supported La Follette. For a short period, during the so-called era of unprecedented prosperity, the Federation became definitely capitalistic, championing big business and catering to it. After it began to feel the effects of the depression, it wavered and criticized business for its failure to stabilize economic life. Organized labor now endorses complete government intervention in the economic life of the country. This new attitude is nothing but mouthing populist sentiment of social control. Likewise, the Federation has discontinued its condemnation of the dole, and has gone so far as to favor Federal unemployment relief and, finally, compulsory unemployment insurance. Otherwise, it is also being drawn closer to the northern populist group. The railroad unions, as led by the four Brotherhoods, have never repudiated their populist beliefs. They have consistently supported the La Follette–Norris group, in the Northwest, and the Wilson-Bryan-McAdoo followers elsewhere. At present the unions, with a few insignificant exceptions, are ardent champions of President Roosevelt and his vague populist program. While the union leaders may still hesitate, there is no doubt that the rank and file are sufficiently wrought up to follow an independent populist movement like that of the 1890's.

The economic situation in the United States is admittedly tragic. It is evident that the present economic unbalance has upset the old equilibrium. But whether conditions will reach such a desperate state that the bulk of the people will readily break, abruptly and violently, with their established and cherished mores is yet uncertain. Assuming that the decline of the business cycle will stop short of catastrophe, the drift in the United States will be toward democratic rather than fascist populism, and less rapidly toward socialism because the bulk of the American workers are imbued with a populist sentiment. The evidences that populism is reviving are unmistakable. It was the dominant issue in the last presidential campaign. Not wishing to alienate all the industrial and financial interests, Roosevelt cautiously tried to strike a balance. Nevertheless, he talked primarily of the "forgotten man" in guarded populist terminology. The growth of populist sentiment is further manifested by the attitude of the House of Representatives during the 1933 session. This body has, since the World War, been ultraconservative. It was the Senate that showed radical tendencies. Now the House has suddenly become the champion of populist ideas, as is shown by its position on the sales tax, unemployment relief, its demand that loans be made to the "small" man by the Reconstruction Finance Corporation, and so on. President Roosevelt's policies since his inauguration, whether they remain permanent features of our life or will ultimately be abandoned, are distinctly of a populist flavor. It is inconceivable that an out-and-out capitalist government would resort to such policies. The criticism which is directed toward the Rooseveltian program by financiers, industrialists, and such politicians as former Secretary of the Treasury Ogden L. Mills, is proof positive.

As the situation crystallizes three types of populism emerge. The least important numerically, and, as usual, the most clear-cut, is the group headed by Professor John Dewey and the League for Independent Political Action. It consists primarily of academic and professional elements, with a sprinkling of the more radical of the other populist groups. It is the democratic "left wing" of the populists, in that it clearly repudiates the two old parties and features a far-reaching social-control program. It is opposed to fundamental compromises with "big business." In the last presidential campaign, it failed to induce other populist elements to join it in organizing a third party, and endorsed Norman Thomas and James Maurer, the Socialist standard bearers. This group may play an important propagandist role, but will only become a serious factor in practical politics when the populist elements decide to launch a "third party" and wage open battle on capitalism. It will undoubtedly resist fascism to the bitter end.

The most substantial populist group, and the one that persisted in its purpose even when populism was at low ebb, is the La Follette-Norris faction. It draws its support chiefly from the midwestern agricultural areas, and is ably flanked by the Farmers Non-Partisan League leaders like Senators Frazier and Nye. Senators Borah and Hiram Johnson are on the fringe of this group, so are Senators Wheeler and Couzens and former Representative, now Mayor, LaGuardia. This faction has always had as its allies the unions of the highly skilled and well-paid workers, as the railroad Brotherhoods and most of the American Federation of Labor unions. It has always espoused organized labor's cause and its legislative program. Occasionally it has even gone beyond the program of organized labor, as in advocating unemployment relief and compulsory unemployment insurance while the Federation of Labor still opposed it. It has consistently stressed economic and political issues of immediate importance to its constituents. Although not fundamentally threatening capitalism, the talk and program of this group have implied an anticapitalist attitude, and from time to time it has sniped at capitalism, as in its demand for government operation of Muscle Shoals and other public utilities. The Plumb Plan for government ownership and control of railroads was distinctly related to its program. It has always been the most consistent element in Congress in fighting for taxation reform that would "relieve the poor man." Only at critical moments did this element, usually with the alliance of organized labor, turn from opportunistic political and economic demands to more radical policies and procedure. In 1924, it ran La Follette on an independent ticket with a moderate populist program that hit at capitalism. At present, this element is for a sober but critical "boring-from-within" the two old parties and does not go beyond regulation of "big business," a more "equitable" taxation, and government aid and protection to farmers and other "small" business interests. The group is championing the interests of the small business man under the NIRA,[1] and is elated over the Tennessee Valley Project. As far as international affairs are concerned, it is most insular, which is a typically liberal-populist-nationalist attitude. (The Dewey group is militantly international—pro-League of Nations, and so on.) It is patriotic, but not chauvinistic. It is nationalistic, but not jingoistic. This moderate populist group will also resist fascism and any other extreme revolutionary attempts. It will probably be the leader in the formation of a pure populist party, as witness the formation of a Progressive party in Wisconsin by the La Follette brothers.

The third populist element has always found its chief base of operation in the southern and southwestern agricultural regions. In bygone days, their spokesmen were "Pitch Fork" Tillman, Tom Watson, Cole Blease, and other such picturesque, loqua-

cious, and showmanlike individuals. Now it is "The Kingfish," Huey Long, and "Alfalfa Bill" Murray who perform for this populist element. This group has shown an extraordinary affinity for the clownish, histrionic type of leader—an affinity which is directly traceable to its general economic instability. Its chief support comes from the "Hill Billies" and their confreres the "poor whites" of urban and rural areas. Populists of this group have always blended religious, moral, and racial issues with their economics and politics. Indeed, these populist elements have usually permitted themselves to be diverted from purely economic issues. Hence, Hitler, who represents the same group psychologically, has subordinated his economic program to chauvinistic and racial issues. Bryan, who was probably the outstanding and the most "sophisticated" spokesman of this southern populist type, gradually became more absorbed in prohibition and fundamentalism. This, volatile populist element also sponsored Ku Klux Klanism, with its anti-Catholic, anti-Negro, anti-Jew, and anti-foreigner program. There was a similar undercurrent in the East and West following the war, but it did not reach such proportions as in the South. Bryan, not being a charlatan like Hitler, did not encourage this element, but he gave a respectable front to intolerance from another angle. His yokel followers fought specific racial and religious groups. The urbane Bryan fought abstract science and demon rum.

La Follette and the northwestern populists, representing the more economically stable and less provincial middle-class elements, refused to be diverted from economic issues. They all condemned religious and racial intolerance, although they could have profited from it. In some of their strongholds the anti-Catholic undercurrent got beyond their control. In Wisconsin, some of La Follette's ablest followers were defeated, even during the greatest La Follette landslides,

---

[1] National Industrial Recovery Act.—Ed.

because they were Catholics. While the unstable populist elements have resorted to "hooliganism" in various forms—tar and feathering, burning crosses, lynching, and so on—the stable middle-class elements have never stooped to such practices. In so far as these stable middle-class elements expressed themselves on moral issues, as prohibition, they did so in a dignified manner. While their restraint is primarily traceable to their relative economic stability, there are important secondary factors. The cosmopolitan influence of the large cities, reinforced by the fact that most of their followers are immigrants or their descendants, who still recall their experience with intolerance and even persecution at home and in this country, served as broadening and restraining factors.

The unstable populist element, although unorganized and relatively inarticulate, is now finding recruits all over the country. There are some organized groups that show symptoms of populism and that may ultimately espouse a full-fledged populist program. Many of the Democratic Party groups in the South are of this nature. If the situation becomes more critical, the remnants of the Bonus Expeditionary Force and its "Khaki Shirt" offshoot are likely to become a strong populist nucleus of fascist tendencies. Similarly, Father Cox's "Green Shirts" and Hunger Marchers, as well as certain elements in the American Legion, will naturally gravitate towards a fascist populism. The state militia units and other such elements may also join in the chorus—and Father Coughlin may yet prove to be an outstanding fascist leader. These groups represent not only the unemployed and the war veterans, but most of the desperately destitute of all walks of life that are not enrolled under the banners of socialism and communism.

In this group are found the potential fascists of the United States. Those with a fascist turn of mind will look to them for leadership. They will provide the shock troops of fascism.

Because of their polyglot composition, racial and religious issues may be subordinated instead of featured, as in Austria and Germany. Since emotional, non-economic issues are essential to such a group they may feature chauvinistic and moral issues. Certain economic issues like the bonus and taxation may receive considerable attention. This new development will present an admirable field for adventurers, who will probably succumb to capitalistic influence, more because of a lack of moral stamina or a lack of understanding of the fundamental philosophy of their cause, than because they are capitalist agents in disguise.

In the light of current events, what course is this populist revival likely to pursue? Even assuming that conditions will grow worse, a revolution is hardly imminent in the United States. In that case, the prospect for a fascist coup is remote. For the present, the only powerfully organized force in the United States is that of the capitalists. Unless the middle-class fascist elements organize and take control in case of collapse, the capitalistic interests will have a clear field. A dictatorship in the United States would have to have the support of at least the capitalists as the most influential force in the country. Thus far this element has been content without a dictatorship. In so far as it is interested in strong government, it wishes to control the unruly and the ultraradical. In view of the Italian experience, where capital is rigidly controlled, and the German experience, where it is seriously hampered, it is questionable whether capitalistic interests in the United States will want a populist-fascist dictatorship unless there is no other way out. They will certainly oppose an economic dictatorship. Should a dictatorship become unavoidable, it would seem that the capitalists would favor a political dictatorship. An economic dictatorship would mean using the state to control themselves. It is certain that, as a first step, the large capitalistic interests would resort to every means possible to control the economic situation through their own established agencies. The reorganization of the Iron and Steel Institute and the featuring of the Swope Plan point the way. Thus, if conditions bring on a dictatorship in the United States it would be a new species of fascism, namely, capitalist-fascism. The difference between capitalist-fascism and populist-fascism is that the former will favor only a purely political dictatorship, with government aid to industry, finance and commerce, whereas populist-fascism favors an inclusive social dictatorship with government control of all important life activities, including the economic.

Recent events have generally demonstrated that fascism is the populist reaction to desperate economic conditions. Capitalism may subsidize it as a countermove to socialism and communism, and it may even support it, but it is not in accord with its philosophy. In a period of collapse, when there is a populist resurgence, capitalism, because it cannot swing the elections, makes the most of the situation by throwing in its lot with fascism or moderate populism. It then trusts to its economic power and its ingenuity to control the situation when the whirlwind has blown over. So far there are few evidences of an organized fascist movement in the United States, although there are scattered elements that have the makings of such a movement. Moreover, it is certain that the dominant capitalistic interests in the United States are not enthusiastic about a fascist dictatorship. At best, capitalism, in so far as it controls the situation, will want a political dictatorship, in order to protect property against either unruly uprisings or ultraradical legislation. Thus, should this country be threatened by an economic collapse, we are likely to witness an attempt at a capitalist-fascist coup rather than a populist-fascist coup.

Since the world political drift is in the direction of populism, the middle class has it in its power to dominate, or at least control, the situation. Its weakness in the United States lies, however, in that its forces are scattered, lacking an effectively organized expression. Similarly, its leaders have thus far failed to manifest the daring and imagination essential for coping with the complicated and chaotic conditions. It is even questionable whether the scattered and confused populist elements can take effective advantage of the drift in their direction. Because of their vacillation in a critical period, they will undoubtedly lose most of those inclined to follow them to charlatans and adventurers. Moreover, these unstable and unorganized populist elements, lacking a fundamental knowledge of social questions and philosophies, will undoubtedly become the prey of adventurers and capitalistic interests. To be sure, President Roosevelt has demonstrated great qualities of leadership, but by trying to balance himself between capitalism and populism, and by using the machinery of one of the old parties, he may find himself ultimately frustrated. There is some evidence that President Roosevelt is trying to crystallize the populist elements in the Democratic Party. There are also indications that the La Follettes will join with the more progressive labor and farmer organizations in the formation of a new party. Should either of these groups succeed in organizing the populist elements, it will make the populist movement more articulate. Even if there were two or more rival populist political organizations, they would still exercise more power than the populist elements exercise now, without clear-cut organizations.

At any rate, the populist elements in the United States have not, since the Spanish-American War, played the significant role that their prototypes have in Europe and in other parts of the world. In part, this fact is explained by their failure to maintain a separate political organization. Previous to the Spanish-American War, they were intermittently organized separately on the political field. This period of organization culminated in the People's Party. But the Democratic Party, which as the minority party, always catered to dissident elements, captured them. This party might have become the middle-class party if it had not been for the conditions created by the Spanish-American War, which diverted the attention of the middle class from fundamental social and economic problems. Following that came a period of economic expansion, with its prosperity, which tended to allay unrest and discontent. Economic conditions, as a result of the crisis of 1907, gave the middle class a new stimulus, so that just before the last war the moderate middle-class elements again came into the ascendancy in the Democratic Party, through the strategy of Bryan, with the nomination of Wilson. The war hysteria diverted the attention of the people, and following the war came the unprecedented period of so-called prosperity. In between that war and that prosperity, there was another attempt to organize separately on the part of the populists, when La Follette in 1924 contested the presidential election. The two most recent attempts at building a middle-class party were frustrated by war and prosperity. There were other incidental factors. The Civil War tradition established certain party prejudices which kept some of the more articulate populist elements out of the Democratic Party. In the Northwest, the populist elements (progressives and farmer non-partisan leaguers) remained in the Republican Party. In this manner the populists were scattered.

Earlier efforts to bring the rural Negro into the political life of the nation have been ignored. JACK ABRAMOWITZ (b. 1918) is one of the few historians who has concerned himself with the role of the Negro in the agrarian reform movement. In the following article he emphasizes the aggressive measures adopted by third-party whites in seeking to integrate the Negro into the political life of the Populist party and the nation. After reading this selection the student should determine whether the Negroes embracing Populism were following in the footsteps of Frederick Douglass, William E. B. DuBois or Booker T. Washington.*

Jack Abramowitz

The Negro and the Populist Movement

By 1890 the Southern Alliance boasted of its alleged three million members and the Colored Alliance asserted it had 750,000 adult male members, 300,000 females, and 150,000 youths. Acting separately and jointly these Alliances stirred the South and carried the hope of an economic and social regeneration of the region.

The interest of Negroes in the Alliance movement and the rapid spread of the organization through the South soon made it imperative that the Southern Alliance win Negro farmers as allies in the common struggle for reform. Contrary to the general assumption that the Colored Alliance was a mere "appendage" of the Southern Alliance, there were serious differences between the two organizations, particularly over the issue of the Lodge Bill or Force Bill as it was known in the South. Despite these barriers a path to unity was laid out in 1890 and in December both Alliances met in convention in Ocala, Florida. At these meetings a program of joint, united action was mapped out, and "it was mutually and unanimously agreed to unite . . . upon the basis adopted December 5, 1890."

The virtual fusion of the two organizations

* From Jack Abramowitz, "The Negro in the Populist Movement," first published in *The Journal of Negro History*, XXXVIII (July, 1953), 257–279, 281–289, by the Association for the Study of Negro Life and History. Footnotes omitted.

made the Alliance a real force in Southern life, but it soon became evident that no major reforms would be effected unless it went into politics. This issue of political action was a source of conflict between Negro and white alliancemen and created serious problems. Most Southern Alliance leaders were strongly Democratic and desired to win that party to the Alliance program. The Colored Alliance was hostile to Southern Democracy and its platform of white supremacy. Negro alliancemen generally looked to the Republicans for political guidance though there was a growing conviction that the party was turning from the Negro and his problems. Within both Alliances there were also substantial forces that favored the creation of an independent third party. This latter movement made rapid headway after 1890 when it became clear that neither Democrats nor Republicans intended instituting a program of genuine agrarian reform. . . .

Like the white alliancemen, the Colored Alliance first tried to influence a major party, in this case the Republicans. Early in September, 1890, the *Atlanta Constitution* cited the "curious fact" that Negro alliancemen in South Carolina were not entering politics, but less than two weeks later said, "the Afro-American Farmers' Alliance is following the footsteps of his white brother and is going into politics." The article went on to say that the Colored Alliance was exerting pressure on Republicans to name the president of the state Colored Alliance, W. A. Grant, for Congress in the First District. In Georgia, too, the Colored Alliance entered politics through the Republican party and an Allianceman named Lectured Crawford was elected to the Assembly from McIntosh County in 1890 and 1892.

The fact that the Colored Alliance seemed to be directing its political energies to the task of reforming the Republicans and was creating some disunity within that party seems to have dulled the edge of Southern fears of the Negro in politics, and the *Atlanta Constitution* calmly headlined its story on the 1890 Ocala convention with the declaration, "Black and white will unite in stamping out sectionalism. The Colored Alliance in Ocala ready to join a third party which will lead to the welfare of the farmer." . . .

At the conclusion of the Ocala conventions of the Alliances in December, 1890, a call was issued for a conference to be held in Cincinnati on February 20, 1891, to discuss the question of a third party. The conference date was later shifted to May 19, 1891, and there were about 1,400 delegates present representing, among others, the Northern Alliance, Southern Alliance, Colored Alliance, Knights of Labor, and the Union Labor party. Nothing much was accomplished because of the hesitancy of the Southern Alliance which wished first to explore all possible avenues of approach to the Democratic party. The Southern delegation was small and when some of them tried to introduce segregation of Colored Alliancemen the convention defeated them by overwhelming vote. They also failed to prevent the conference from establishing a tentative People's Party committee which was to exist pending the formation of a permanent party organization for the 1892 elections. The inability of the Southerners to prevent establishment of this temporary committee meant that a third party virtually was assured within the next year. . . .

The Cincinnati conference had endeavored to guarantee the founding of a third party, but there were other forces working for the same end. In January, 1891, a conference of the Alliances and sympathetic groups had set up a Conference of Industrial Organizations in Washington, D. C., and this organization sent out a call for a convention in St. Louis on February 22, 1892, where all interested groups were to discuss the issue of a national third party. Though few in numbers the Negro delegation to this convention included some of the most active members of the Colored Alliance. . . .

At the St. Louis convention the Negro delegation proved a spirited group and was active in the work of the assemblage. The resistance of white Southern delegates had again stymied the meeting preventing a clear cut stand on the third party issue, but this was overcome by the strategy of waiting until the convention adjourned and then reconvening as a mass meeting to discuss the third party issue. . . .

The St. Louis convention had set the stage for the formalities required to establish a national party, but the agrarian insurgents did not wait upon the niceties of political custom. As early as 1890 there were Alliance parties, People's parties, or Union Labor parties in nearly all Mid-Western and Southern states. It was increasingly evident that the independent political movement was moving into high gear.

The potentialities awaiting the Populist movement, should it seek to win the Negro vote and integrate the Negro in the party itself, were first discernible in Kansas where there was less tradition of anti-Negro sentiment to hinder this development. In their 1890 convention the Kansas Populists, then widely known as the Alliance party, named the Reverend Benjamin F. Foster, a Negro minister of Topeka, as candidate for state Auditor. The Populist state ticket was the result of a fusion of Union Laborites, Alliancemen, and Democrats, and it was generally believed that the nomination of a Negro for the post of auditor was designed to win Negroes away from the Republican party. . . .

The results of this new approach were evident in the election returns which saw the Republican majority reduced to about 15,000 compared to the previous 82,000. Foster ran six thousand votes *ahead* of the ticket and received 112,000 votes. This impressive display of strength increased demands by Negro Re-publicans that their party plan to put a Negro on the ticket in 1892. These pleas again fell on deaf ears, but an effort was made to mollify Negro feelings by the appointment of John L. Waller to the Madagascar consulate, a move that pacified the Kansas political scene but added more turmoil to the national scene when Waller was imprisoned later by the French on charges of aiding a local revolutionary movement. . . .

The extent to which Negroes continued to function within the Kansas populist movement is not clear, but it is known that the Kansas delegation to the founding of the national People's Party in Omaha in 1892 included at least one Negro member, and the party made sufficient headway in Negro districts to occasion a comment from an anti-Populist Negro paper in November, 1892 that "it was reported that in some sections of the state there were breaks in the solid colored voters towards the People's party." . . .

Though Kansas was one of the first to appeal directly for the Negro vote, other states were not long in following suit. Arkansas independents had pointed the way when the Union Labor party nominated a Negro, the Reverend I. P. Langley, for Congress from the 2nd District in 1890. In 1892 the state convention wrote into its platform the resolution of Negro delegate I. Glopsy, "That it is the object of the People's party to elevate the downtrodden irrespective of race or color." In Louisiana the People's party held its first convention in Alexandria on February 1, 1892, and there were twenty-four Negroes among the delegates. The leader of the Negro delegation, C. A. Roachborough, was nominated for State Treasurer but withdrew his name.

Texas, the founding state of both the Southern and the Colored Alliance, showed an early tendency toward Negro-white cooperation. A Populist state convention in Dallas on August 17, 1891, named two Negroes to the party's executive committee and Negroes remained on the committee until 1900.

The new party must have made strong efforts to win Negro members, for its 1892 convention heard a report from delegates from some of the southern counties "that the colored people are coming into the new party in squads and companies. They have colored third party speakers and are organizing colored clubs." . . .

Texas Populism was only mildly successful in 1892, and its coalition with the dissident Democratic element known as the Jeffersonian Democrats won only eight seats in the legislature. In 1894 the coalition was more successful and captured twenty-two of the 128 seats. The degree to which the Texas third party actually attracted Negroes may never be known but the significance of the open appeal made for Negro votes cannot be overlooked.

Indicative of the effort to win Negro support was the summoning of Negroes for jury duty in Nacogdoches County by the Populist sheriff, an act that incurred the displeasure of some elements in the county. Such actions undoubtedly stimulated the early interest of Texas Negroes in the party. Mention has already been made of the presence of Negroes at the founding of the state party, and the files of the *Southern Mercury* give additional evidence of substantial Negro participation in the movement. In August, 1892, the paper published a one-column lead article by a Negro, P. K. Chase, titled, "The Colored Man and Politics," which declared, "The one and only advantageous political course of the Negro, under present existing affairs is to support the people's party." He then went on to say wishfully, "The people's party is not heard to say that 'this is a white man's government' but that this is a people's government."

Mr. Chase was not accurate in his estimate of the views of Populist leaders on the race question, for evidence will be given later to show that certain party leaders were not unwilling to use the race issue in a futile effort to avoid the Democratic characterization of "Negro lover." The sincerity of the Populists on the race issue was not, however, the main obstacle to winning Negro adherents. A stronger impediment was the able and vigorous leadership given the Texas Republican party by a corps of Negroes, particularly Norris Wright Cuney. During the very period when the People's party was trying to win the Negro vote, Cuney was leading the fight against the "lily-white" Republican faction. It is conceivable that many Negroes who might otherwise have joined the People's party felt compelled to aid Cuney in his losing battle against those seeking to subvert the Republican party. Cuney was opposed to Populism, but he did favor a fusion ticket in 1896 and was able to beat off the opposition of the "lily-whites" on the issue. This was his last victory, for the opposition took over the party later that year and he died in 1898.

Though Cuney, the outstanding leader of Texas Negroes, remained outside the third party the Populists did make a notable conversion in John B. Rayner who served as spokesman for Negro Populists from 1894 to 1898. Rayner was born a slave in 1850 in North Carolina and had attended schools in that state after the Civil War. During the 1870's he was elected a sheriff's deputy, and in 1881 he moved to Texas where he served as a teacher and preacher. Though originally a Republican he left the party in the 1890's and joined the third party. At the 1894 state convention he was on the Committee on Platforms and Resolutions and in 1895 and 1896 he served on the executive committee of the Texas People's party. A fearless and capable agitator, he stumped the countryside for the party and "took his life in his hands when he went into certain counties of East Texas." His work was described as "organizing colored Populist clubs, himself, and directing the work of a corps of colored assistants. Up

and down the state he roamed, to the ut-
termost limits of the negro empire, preaching
always the doctrine of Populism, with special
reference to the hope which it held for the
colored man." . . .

The appeal to the Negro and the appearance of Negroes in prominent posts in the
third party resulted in a change of tone by
Southern editors who had heretofore been
prone to regard Populism as an essentially
Western innovation. In Georgia the *Atlanta
Constitution* had viewed the third party
complacently in early 1891, but the headway
made by the Populists led to a startling
change of attitude before the year ended.
When President Polk of the Southern Alliance appeared with General Weaver,
"Sockless" Jerry Simpson, and others at an
Atlanta Alliance rally in July, 1891, the press
bitterly attacked the third party moves. By
August the Atlanta *Journal* was fulminating
against the "trio of communists and south
haters"—Messrs. Lease, Simpson, and
Weaver.

As the 1892 election drew closer the Georgia press became nearly hysterical in its efforts to turn back the new movement, the con-
sequences of which had been so completely
overlooked the year before. When a long time
Democrat, Seaborn Wright, was offered the
Populist nomination for Congress in the 7th
District, the *Atlanta Constitution* warned
editorially: "Don't do it, Mr. Wright. For,"
concluded the editor, "to accept the nomination of a party which is blatantly opposed
to democracy, and which has for its purpose
the division of the white vote will be to place
himself outside the democratic organization.
Don't do it. Mr. Wright. Don't!"

The overwrought tones of the editor were
justified for in that critical period of Georgia
history it must have seemed to the old line
political bosses that their house was being
blown apart by the Populist gale. The Georgia Alliance had been captured for the third
party by young Tom Watson, and the threat

of the new party was a grim reality. In their
battle against this insurgency the Democrats
fired all their volleys and warned that a Populist victory would bring Negro supremacy,
race mongrelism, and the destruction of the
Saxon womanhood of wives and daughters.

The reason for such an unbridled appeal to
race hate is not difficult to ascertain. In a
word, it was the strenuous and successful
effort of the Watson forces to unite the Negro
vote with that of the poor white. Typical of
Watson's approach was a speech he made to
Negroes of his district during the 1892 campaign:

I want you colored citizens to draw near that
you may hear what I have got to say for I have
something to say to you especially. . . . It is a well
known fact that when I ran for the legislature in
1882, the black people supported me almost to a
man. . . . I was hounded down and abused because
I stood up at the courthouse and thanked you for
giving me your support. I said that I could see no
reason why, because a man was colored, he should
not have his say as to who was the representative
from McDuffie county as well as the proudest
white man. Now I want to say another thing to you
and what I say to you I want to say in public in the
blaze of day. I pledge you my word and honor that
if you stand up for your rights and for your
manhood, if you stand shoulder to shoulder with us
in this fight, you shall have fair play and fair
treatment as men and as citizens, irrespective of
your color. (Great cheering) . . . My friends, this
campaign will decide whether or not your people
and ours can daily meet in harmony, and work for
law, and order, and morality, and wipe out the
color line and put every man on his citizenship
irrespective of color.

This daring and outspoken appeal for the
Negro vote was reinforced by Watson's
speeches to white audiences where he would
"pledge the white listeners to defend the
Negro's constitutional rights, making them
hold up their hands and promise." These efforts to secure Negro-white unity were
carried through to the lowest levels of the
party and on one occasion, in Greene County,

the local Populists placed five Negroes on the campaign committee, an act that brought much comment and criticism. . . .

The courageous stand taken by Watson won him active support from many Negroes including the Reverend H. S. Doyle, a Negro preacher of outstanding ability and incredible courage. In the 1892 campaign he delivered sixty-three speeches in Watson's behalf despite many attempts on his life. On one occasion he was forced to flee to Watson's home for protection, and Watson sent out a call to his supporters to defend Doyle from threatened lynching. The response was such that "all that day and the next night farmers continued to assemble until 'fully two thousand' Populists crowded the village—arms stacked on Watson's veranda. The farmers remained on guard for two nights."

The spectacle of masses of "wool hat boys" rallying to the defense of a Negro was truly suggestive of the revolution taking place in Georgia life, but the old line politicians knew how to save the day. Reckless and unfounded charges of "Negro domination" whipped doubting whites into line; outright fraud at the polls secured dubious majorities; and force and violence removed "notorious" Negroes to such an extent that it was estimated at least fifteen Negroes were killed by Democrats in the 1892 election. The result of such activity was the victory of the Democrats by a 70,000 vote majority in the October state elections and the defeat of Watson in the November polling.

Failure to win did not diminish the enthusiasm of the state Populists who now began to gear their work toward the 1894 elections. Once again they appealed to the Negro voter and this time it would seem they achieved considerable success. It is strange that the 1894 election in Georgia has not received fuller attention to date, for there is little question that the results demonstrated the outstanding success of Populist tactics. The *Atlanta Constitution* devoted nearly a full

page in its October 4 and 5 issues to the results and in nearly every county carried by the Populists it was reported that the victory was the result of Negro votes. Even if one allows for the efforts of the dominant party to portray the third party as the "Negro party" it must be stated that the reports reflect a strong measure of Negro support for the party. . . .

Despite the appreciable gain in Populist voting strength Watson failed to win the Congressional seat, but this time the frauds were so obvious that his opponent felt honor bound to resign and run again in a new election. Though Watson was again defeated in the special election, the menace of the Populist vote led the Democratic majority in the legislature to set up a new registration law in December, 1894, which established district committees on which the Democrats outvoted the Populists two to one. The committees regulated registration and ensured Democratic control of that important phase of the elective franchise, a vital factor in enabling them to "count out" the Negro vote.

In 1896 the Democrats did not have to repeat such crudities as awarding a candidate a majority of 13,780 in a district of 11,240 voters! With the registration machinery firmly in their hands and with the Populist party split over the fusion with the Bryan forces, the state machine rode roughshod over the third party. After 1896 the Populists were finished as a major force in the state and little remained of that remarkable time in Georgia history which has been best described in Woodward's assertion that "never before or since have the two races in the South come so close together politically."

The efforts of Populists in the South and mid-West to integrate the Negro into the party did not pass unnoticed by the Negro press. The *Wisconsin Afro-American*, an influential mid-Western Negro paper, wrote approvingly of the work of women in Alliance and Populist groups and urged Negro women to enter the same work. It also commended the Populists for nominating and electing the first Negro to hold office in Wisconsin. The *Huntsville Gazette* of Alabama also surveyed the political scene in the South and noted cryptically, "Alliance is moving onward and Democracy trembles in its boots." . . .

This new approach to politics by Southerners, many of whom had previously held to the hope that the Democrats might be won over to Populism, was not achieved without considerable hesitation and many misgivings. The difficulties inherent in any attempt to unite Negroes and whites in the face of years of institutionalized hostility are best reflected in two excerpts from the convention proceedings at Omaha:

"T. P. Lloyd, a confederate from Southern Florida was called to the front.
" 'When on my way here,' he said, 'I was asked whom I favored for president. I said Fred Douglass. When they got over their astonishment, and asked me why, I explained that if we were going to have nigger domination in the south the sooner the better. I want to know if there is a soldier here, federal or confederate, who thinks there is any danger of nigger rule.' (cries of 'no')"

Two days later in the course of heavy debate the following incident occurred:

"A Kansas delegate moved the previous question, but the chairman stated that a 'colored brother' desired to say a few words. 'I won't yield to any brother,' said the Kansan. . . . The resolution was then adopted. . . . The colored delegate now protested. . . . 'I don't think it is right,' said he, 'that after you all have spoken, you should call the previous question. (Laughter) You expect us to help you out with our votes.' (Applause)". . .

Negroes may not have enjoyed hearing the old canard that this or that white man knew how "to control and handle" them, but the possibilities of the new political alignment under the leadership of the third party led to hope of advance in the future. Even that arch enemy of Kansas Populism, the *Parsons Weekly Blade,* felt the new party might justify its existence if it removed certain odious Democratic office holders from Missouri politics.

The vigor with which the third party men had undertaken to win the Negro vote did not mean People's party leaders were free from anti-Negro practices. With the Democrats raising the cry of "Negro lover" against them the Populists sought to deny the charge by establishing themselves as the "white man's party." This was especially true in the early days before the party leadership became fully wakened to the powerful weapon of Negro-white cooperation. In this early period the party leaders made Frederick Douglass their target for abuse. In July, 1892, the *Southern Mercury* quoted the Goldthwait *Advocate* in asking, "Do you forget how Cleveland invited Fred Douglass, the negro, and white wife to receptions in Washington? Negro social equality beats any force bill. . . . Go with the party that does place the negro where he belongs, giving him his rights under law, and nothing more." On September 22, the paper continued its attack on Douglass by referring to him as "the notorious negro with a white wife" and denouncing the Democrats for staying with Cleveland after his cordiality to Douglass. . . .

While the Populists adopted the program of fusion in many states, their outstanding success was achieved in North Carolina. Populism had an early start in that state because of the strong support of the Alliances and the gradual conversion to Populism of Leonidas Polk, editor and president of the Southern Alliance. Though a staunch Democrat all his life, Polk was becoming disillusioned with the chances of reform through that party. In fact, he was being boomed for the Populist nomination for President when his sudden death in 1892 removed what might well have been the greatest political threat to the Democratic "solid South." . . .

The relatively enlightened attitude of the party toward the Negro was a carry over of the friendly relations begun by the Alliances. In 1891 Polk's newspaper, the *Progressive Farmer,* had underscored Southern Alliance sympathy for the Negro by stating that when it requested more educational facilities in North Carolina "we want it understood that we embrace in this appeal to our General Assembly the negro children of the state." The new party exhibited a similar spirit and the interest of Negroes in the movement was demonstrated when General Weaver spoke in Raleigh during the 1892 campaign. He "was escorted to Brookside Park by 300 white men and fifty negroes, all on horseback." Though Negroes exhibited interest in the movement the Populists did not bid openly for their vote at first. Even so the newly formed party did very well in its debut in 1892, polling 47,000 votes of a total of 274,000 and electing eleven members of the state legislature.

By 1894 the Populists had come to recognize the value of fusion and after toying with the idea of joining the Democrats they set up a joint ticket with the state Republicans. In addition, they courted the vote of reform Democrats by endorsing the Democratic candidate for the state Supreme Court, Walter Clark. Though Clark remained a Democrat he was widely respected among all sections of the electorate and his views were very close to those of the Populists. The respectability gained by this endorsement plus the coalition effected with the Republicans enabled the fusionists to sweep the legislature.

During the period of fusion control significant reforms were enacted. In addition, hundreds of Negroes were appointed or elected to local offices and the size of the electorate expanded from 278,000 to a total of 330,000 as the restrictive laws of the Democratic regimes were cast aside and election rather than appointment of local officials was made general.

In 1896 the North Carolina Populists achieved the ultimate in political ambidexterity by endorsing Bryan, a Democrat, for President, running a Populist for Governor, and fusing with the Republicans for state offices. This bewildering condition was rivaled by the result of the election which found the Democrats carrying the state for the Presidency, the Republicans winning the Governorship, and the fusionists triumphant in the state legislature. For the fourth time since the Civil War a Negro, George C. White, was elected from the state to serve in Congress.

The victory of the fusionists roused the Democrats to action to forestall any repetition of the maneuver in 1898. Furnifold M. Simmons, new Democratic leader of the state, undertook a vigorous campaign aimed at splitting the alliance between Populists and Republicans. Sounding the tocsin of "white supremacy" he proceeded energetically to rally the Democratic party to the task of driving the Negro out of politics. In this battle no holds were barred and even a representative of genteel Southern womanhood might write, "It is time for the shotgun to play a part, and an active one, in the elections." Southern chivalry saw nothing shocking in the added assertion, "We applaud to the echo your determination that our old heroic river shall be choked with the bodies of our enemies white and black, but what the state shall be redeemed."

The press was virtually unanimous in denouncing the fusionists and young Josephus Daniels converted his *News and Observer* into a veritable hate sheet, publishing reckless charges of "Negro domination" and inciting the white population against the Negroes. The much vaunted dislike for "outsiders" by the local population was overlooked and "Pitchfork Ben" Tillman came from South Carolina to give first-hand advice on how to bar the Negro from the polls. In his wake there rose a crop of organizations aping the tactics of the South Carolina Red Shirts.

The result of this activity coupled with the national debacle of Populism in 1896 brought on a split in the fusion ranks in the 1898 election and the Democrats rode to victory. Within forty-eight hours of their triumph the evil seed sown by Simmons, Daniels, Tillman, and their followers bore fruit in the Wilmington riot, a holocaust of death and destruction in which scores of Negroes were beaten and killed by a hate crazed mob. Their purpose accomplished, the Democratic leaders now piously professed shock but withal held to the belief that it was the fault of the "intolerable" conditions of Negro "domination." In far off Dayton, Ohio, a young Negro poet looked askance as the victory of hate and the carnage it had wrought and cried,

> Loud, from the South, Damascan cries
> Fall on our ears, unheeded still.
> No helping powers stir and rise.
> Hate's opiate numbs the nation's will.
> Slumbers the North (while Honor dies!)
> Soothed by the insidious breath of lies.

While the North slept the Democrats pushed through a state constitutional amendment in 1899 that virtually disfranchised the Negro. If the amendment was adopted by methods highly suggestive of wholesale fraud, the means were overlooked in deference to the nobility of the ends served. North Carolina had again been "redeemed." This time the Negro was effectively barred from any future alliance with the poor white by a legislative requirement of a literacy test which acted to keep Negroes from the ballot box. . . .

So far as Negroes were concerned they were bound to be attracted to a party that bid openly for their support, particularly when the Republicans were moving in the direction of a lily-white party in the South. Frederick Douglass was not unaware of the work of the Populists, but he remained true to the old party and just before his death in 1895 he

wrote that "We have a chance of getting a better man from the Republicans than from the Democrats or Populists." The younger element in Negro life was not so firmly rooted in the Republican tradition and might have been won over. In his recollections of the period Dr. William E. B. DuBois recalls he was not favorably impressed by the Populists but by 1896 he "began now to believe (populism) was a third party movement of deep significance."

The success of the Populist appeal to the Negro voter plus coalitions with the insurgent element in the region held high promise for the political future of the party in the South. The acceptance of Bryan in 1896 wrecked their hopes by tying them to the dominant political machine of the South and cluttering up the campaign with the confusing issue of free silver, an issue that ought properly have had only marginal importance. Paul Dunbar probably expressed the sentiment of many Negroes on the silver question when he wrote in October, 1896:

> An' hit ain't de so't o' money dat is pesterin' my min',
> But de question I want ansewehed's how to get at any kin'!

To Negro Populists the prospect of fusion with the Democrats was a disaster since it would lead inevitably to the destruction of the new relationship that had begun to develop during the period of insurgency. Henry Demarest Lloyd understood this when he wrote, "The Democrats, the 'classes,' hate the new people who have dared to question the immemorial supremacy of their aristocratic rule, and who have put into actual association, as not even the Republicans have done, political brotherhood with the despised negro."

The handful of Negroes at the St. Louis convention in 1896 joined the old line white reformers of the South in a vain effort to save the Populist party. Lloyd wrote touchingly that "the most eloquent speeches made were those of whites and blacks explaining to the convention what the rule of the Democrats meant in the South. A delegate from Georgia, a coal black Negro, told how the People's party alone gave full fellowship to his race." It was at this convention, too, that S. D. Walton, a Negro delegate, seconded the nomination of Tom Watson for Vice-President because, "He has made it possible for the black man to vote according to his conscience in Georgia."

More than fifty years after the St. Louis convention a white delegate from Iowa, A. W. Ricker, recalled the presence of Negro delegates from the South, one of whom spoke vigorously against the proposed unity with the Democrats whom he described as a type of crayfish—"When you come alongside of it you can't tell if you met him or overtook him."

The advice and pleas of these people went unheeded and the party moved swifty to its doom. The collapse of Populism in 1896 put an end to a movement that had every chance of producing a truly emancipated South in which the Negro would have been accorded a respectable position which might in time have broken down hostility and suspicion between Negro and white.

With the smash-up of Populism and the loss of hope of reform through active and aggressive political activity, and with the right to vote suppressed by a vindictive band of demagogues, the direction of Negro leadership became confused. Out of this confusion were created the circumstances that made possible the rise of Booker T. Washington and his philosophy.

Of the contemporary economists who opposed the Populists on the intellectual front, FRANK LeROND McVEY (1869-1953) was the only one who prepared a monograph about them. Most of his writings cut across the fields of government, education, and economics. *"The Populist Movement"* appeared at a crucial time—in the presidential year of 1896. Except for a few state studies, articles, and essays of varying quality, it was the only general treatment of the subject until the appearance of *The Populist Revolt* by John Hicks in 1931. The following selection, which analyzes the sources of Populist strength and weakness, is representative of the unsympathetic conservative views of those who fought Populism during the 1890s. This line of reasoning carried into the twentieth century. *

Frank LeRond McVey

Socialistic Tendencies of the People's Party

From reading the accounts of the various Populist conventions, and the speeches of prominent men in the new party, it has been very difficult to determine whether or not the party is socialistic. The action of the conventions indicated one thing, the speeches another. It is true that the Omaha platform was in existence; and yet the continued references to other issues than those raised in that political manifesto gave the impression that the planks were not so universally accepted as had been supposed, and that the whole party was drifting away from them. Such was the belief entertained by the general public; while behind the scenes a battle was being carried on between the silver and socialist elements in the party itself—a one-plank platform versus the Omaha platform. The radicals wished to sustain the latter, while the conservatives desired the party to drop all issues except that of silver and fight only for financial reform. These two elements were at sword's points over the apparent insignificance of silver in the Omaha platform. The radicals were conservative silver men, while the conservatives were radical silverites. The silver men had entered the party more for the purpose of booming silver than to mitigate the wrongs of

---

* From Frank LeRond McVey, "The Populist Movement" in T. N. Carver (comp.), *Selected Readings in Rural Economics* (Boston: Ginn & Company, 1916), pp. 692–698.

the oppressed. The Congress of the United States had passed the Sherman Act[1] and later had repealed it, so that the silver men could hardly expect any support from the old parties. They saw a way out through the new party; but they had not taken into account the real causes of that party's existence, and consequently failed to secure any great advantage for silver. Meantime both Republicans and Democrats have turned like needles to a loadstone in the direction of silver, and the silver men have hurried from the different parties, including the People's, to the neutral grounds where the advocates of this coinage seem universally to be gathering.

This contest has been waged from the very beginning of the party. It began in debates and ended in a party rupture; for the long-expected crisis has now occurred and the true Populistic element has broken away from the silverites, and stands firmly on the Omaha platform.

The leaders of the party favored the silver side of the fight, but the rank and file of Populism was not to be beguiled by any such sentiment. The silver men attempted to undermine the platform, but without success. Every time the question was brought up a contest ensued, in which the silver men were driven to the wall. In the conference of the Populist leaders at St. Louis in December, 1894, a desperate attempt was made to change the Omaha platform, but the great majority of delegates at the conference voted to re-affirm it. Since that time the one-plank silverites have tried to get control of the conventions in Chicago and Cleveland, held for the purpose of nominating city officers. Chicago and Cleveland are strongly Populistic, hence the battles in these two cities were significant of the strength of the two factions in the general party. In Cleveland there was no evidence of any silver element, while in

Chicago the silver champions were forced to remain silent. The same experience has been repeated in the state conventions, and even in the silver states the leaders of this movement were not able to control the Populist Party. The presence of the silver faction has obscured the real purpose of the party to such an extent as to render the question at the head of this chapter [Is the People's Party Socialistic?] a pertinent one. But the defection of this element leaves the originators of the party without the screen of free coinage. The two tendencies have been pointed out, and the student of this party movement can discern the motives without the perplexing presence of cross-purposes.

The government has very materially aided the development of the West. Large sums of money were there spent, and large tracts of land were given away to encourage immigration. The Pacific railroads received both money and land from the government, and states were given thousands of acres for educational purposes. The national government has also built roads and aided in the construction of canals. In addition to all this the Homestead and Pre-emption laws opened large tracts of land which were to be had in small lots for the asking. The legislatures of the various Western states have been very ready to help this or that undertaking, in order to advance the states. All this led to an exaggerated conception of the power of government to accomplish large results in bringing about prosperity. The government's policy has made some men rich, and has also accustomed the people to look toward Washington whenever they were hard pressed or wanted legislation to assist some contemplated enterprise. This reliance upon Washington has passed through various stages, until now it manifests itself in the demand that the government shall own and control the railroads. It is not to be understood that the idea of paternalism in government has of itself developed to the point

[1] The Sherman Silver Purchase Act (1890) required the U.S. government to purchase nearly twice as much silver as before.

of socialism; but the principles of government extension, public ownership and management, have fallen upon ground well prepared for them. The consequence has been a rapid growth of these principles and a general belief in them.

As a result the people of the West are divided into three classes, separated only by their distance from the first, which forms the nucleus of the People's Party. In reality this first class is composed of socialists; the majority would probably admit that they were such. In the second class are to be found many farmers, laborers, business and professional men, who are not Populists, but who favor government ownership of railroads and telegraphs and an extension of government activity. This class fear the word "socialist" and in their hearts regard the socialist as a species of bomb-thrower who is at war with society. Hence they cannot see the similarity between their own belief and that of the socialist. The third class consists of men who repudiate socialism even more plainly than the second, but who are nevertheless declared paternalists.

Such, in the main, is the situation in the West. As a matter of course there are many exceptions, but the large majority of the people belong to one or the other of the classes mentioned. Under such conditions the Populists have naturally received much sympathy, and the very fact that they have had sympathizers has encouraged them to express their views much more forcibly than they would otherwise have done. This fact has also given them sufficient force to hold out against the strategies of the silver men, and by the exhibition of their power to add strength to strength.

Strong as has been the spirit of paternalism in shaping the beliefs and opinions of the West, there has been at work another force, perhaps even more potent and active—that of railroad oppression. The Pacific railroads from the first watered their stocks. The earnings at ordinary rates were insufficient to warrant dividends on the increased capitalization. In order to pay these, an enormous income was necessary, and the only way to obtain this was to impose heavier charges on freight, and for many years this practice was maintained. Although the rates were reduced later, the extortion practiced has caused a hatred of railroads and other corporations. Protests arose from all sides, and the Farmers' Alliance with other similar organizations, shaped the movement until the meeting at Cincinnati in 1891 brought the People's Party into existence. Although there were other material causes of the movement, it was the sentiment of the Western representatives which shaped the platform in regard to railroads and telegraphs, and from this section came much of the socialism introduced into the platform.

The question naturally arises. Why do the socialist papers hurl all kinds of invectives at the new organization and, if it is really socialistic, refuse to consider it worthy to be classed with socialistic parties? A quotation from the *People,* the leading journalistic exponent of that belief in the United States, may cast some light on the question. "The plan of the silverites to make the People's Party more reactionary than it was, has been substantially carried out." So long as the silver element in the party was not predominant, the socialists had no objections to the platform of the Omaha convention; but when financial questions began to overshadow the other planks, then the cry of "We told you so" was raised, and the People's Party was declared to have betrayed the principles set forth in its platform. The *National Watchman* said soon after: "The time for Populism and Socialism to part has come, and those who fail to realize the situation will have, in the future, ample time to reflect upon their error in judgment. What we want now is a clear-cut, aggressive, intelligent propaganda upon financial reform." Even this conservative Populist paper recognized the fact that there is such a thing as socialism in the party. The parting did come at Omaha, but not as then hoped by the writer of the editorial. The silver and financial reform advocates instead of the adherents of the entire platform were forced to retire.

The Omaha platform of the People's Party is a remarkable document in many ways, and one of its peculiarities is the ambiguity encountered at every turn. Its whole tone is socialistic. Yet if the charge of socialism were brought against it, the defender of the platform could at once deny the assertion, and define the section attacked in such a way as to refute the statement. This ambiguity is due to the two opinions prevailing in the convention which framed the platform, and to the endeavor to satisfy both. There was, on the one hand, the real element of the party itself and, on the other, the silver advocates who had been drawn to the new party in the hope of advancing their cause. It was for the purpose of appeasing the more conservative element that the platform was softened in places and the utterances on certain subjects made less positive. But despite the ambiguity of the platform as a whole, there are to be found certain positive declarations of principles which may be compared with the purposes of the socialist. By this means the real similarity of the two views, if there be any, will appear.

Socialist[2]	People's Party
1. Abolition of inheritance in land or other means of production, such as machinery, railroads, telegraphs, and canals.	
2. Abolition of private property in land or any other means of the production of wealth.	
3. Abolition of wages system.	
4. Abolition of competitive system.	
5. National ownership of land.	"The land, including all the natural sources of wealth, is the heritage of the people and should not be monopolized for speculative purposes."
6. National ownership of railroads and telegraphs.	National ownership of telegraphs and railroads.
7. A graded income tax.	A graded income tax.
8. A paper currency of fiat money.	A paper currency or fiat money.
9. Abolition of national banks.	Abolition of national banks.
10. The public lands to be declared inalienable. Revocation of all land grants to corporations or individuals, the conditions of which have not been complied with.	"Alien ownership of land should be prohibited. All lands now held by railroads and other corporations in excess of their actual needs should be reclaimed by the government and held for actual settlers only."
11. Establishment of postal-deposit and savings banks.	"We demand that postal savings banks be established by the government for the safe deposit of the earnings of the people and to facilitate exchange."

---

[2] 10 in platform of Socialist Labor Party of Central Labor Union of Cleveland "Socialism and Universal Suffrage," p. 19.

12. Adoption of constitutional amendment requiring the election of president and vice-president by the direct vote of the people. Also providing for election of the United States senators by direct vote of the people.
13. Rigid enforcement of eight-hour law in all public departments.

14. Adoption of the initiative and of the referendum.

"That we favor a consitional provision limiting the office of president and vice-president to one term and providing for the election of the senators by a direct vote of the people."

"That we demand a rigid enforcement of the existing eight-hour law on government work, and ask that a penalty clause be added to the said law."
"That we commend to the thoughtful consideration of the people and the reform press the legislative system known as the initiative and referendum."

The fourteen demands of socialism have been selected with care and with the desire to secure a representative list of the various principles and tenets set forth by them. They are taken from the planks of the various socialistic parties and truly reflect the opinions of socialism. In comparing the planks of the People's Party platform, we find that nine of them correspond closely to those of the socialists. Such a similarity is not an accident, but the result of thought along the same lines.

The People's Party could not have adopted a platform in so many ways akin to that of the socialists if there had not been a previous tendency in that direction. It is true that the great fundamental principles of common ownership and equality of income are not expressed, nor is the last even hinted; yet the national ownership of the railroad and telegraph, coupled with a demand for increased State action, can only characterize the platform as socialistic in its tendency.

ANNA ROCHESTER (1880–1966), a well-known
left-wing writer, was a former editor of *World Tomorrow*
and employee of the United States Children's Bureau. She
wrote on a wide variety of subjects ranging from children to
capitalism. Her books include *American Capitalism,
1607–1800* (1949), *Capitalism and Progress* (1945), and
Why Farmers Are Poor (1940). *The Populist Movement in
the United States*, from which this selection is taken, was
published in 1943 when the Soviet Union and the United
States were allies. Like others of her persuasion, she
attempted to rewrite American history within a Marxist
framework. She detects certain parallels between Populism
and Soviet socialism. *

Anna Rochester

Populism and Soviet Socialism

Populism appeared when monopoly began
to take on new forms which seriously encroached upon the freedom of capitalist competition. It carried on during the last three
decades of the nineteenth century the struggle
for political democracy which has been an integral part of American life from the period of
the American Revolution to the present war
for survival of the United Nations under
attack from fascist powers. This long historic
struggle has had many high points, symbolized for us by such figures as Thomas Jefferson, Andrew Jackson, and Abraham
Lincoln. But always the work has been
carried forward by the people themselves.

The Populist movement produced no great
leaders but it represented many diverse
groups banded together against the increasingly oppressive power of big business.
Debtors were stirring against the tyranny of
private banking. Farmers were in revolt
against exploitation by industrial interests
which controlled the outlets for their product
and the manufacture of farm equipment.
Wage workers were organizing to protect
themselves on the job and looked to political
action as a normal part of their struggle.

Populism sought to overthrow the "invisible government" by monopoly and finance and to recapture for the masses of

* From Anna Rochester, *The Populist Movement in the United States* (New York: International Publishers,
1943), pp. 120–124. Reprinted by permission of International Publishers Co., Inc. Copyright © 1943.

people—workers, farmers, small producers, small businessmen and professionals—the control of the government. Populist struggles brought certain decisive victories which strengthened our political democracy. And we have now a wealth of information on the workings of monopoly and the power of finance capital within this country, together with a considerable measure of regulation and control.

There are notable achievements, resulting directly from the Populist movement, but they have by no means solved our economic and political problems. They do provide the basis for further progress, and they are worth defending at all costs from attack by fascist forces. They make imperative a quick and decisive victory in the present war with Nazi Germany and Japan. Defense of "government of the people, by the people, and for the people" is our primary concern. To this end, victory in the war against the fascist nations takes precedence over all other issues.

But already people are wondering what kind of world we shall have in this country after the war is over. Will the contrasts of wealth and poverty be further sharpened by war profits, as they were after the First World War? Will there be again terrible periods of mass unemployment and despair?

When this war against fascism is completely won, the American people—workers, farmers, small businessmen, housewives, Negro and white, Jew and Gentile—will be trying to shape a future that is better than the past. That they will be ready to move rapidly toward socialism is extremely doubtful. The Populist tradition is so strong among us and so deeply rooted in the earlier stages of capitalist development that many sincere defenders of democracy and economic security for the masses still seek a revival of the past instead of looking toward a creative future. And no responsible group within the United States would propose or support a minority move, an attempt to "set up" socialism before

the majority of the American people desire it.

In spite of this obviously apparent fact, fear of socialism has long been cultivated by reactionary forces within this country. They do not forget that parallel with the Populist movement there was taking shape an American Socialist movement rooted primarily in the working class. They know very well that the Communist Party of the United States was organized by the forward-looking majority within the old Socialist Party. It carries on the work which was started by Eugene V. Debs more than forty years ago and which, in turn, was rooted in many generations of the American working class.

At various times the servants of finance capital have used Populist measures as sops to quiet popular unrest, as brakes to retard the growth of socialist thinking. Even many who genuinely oppose monopoly and "invisible government" by finance capital raise their voices to misrepresent the nature of socialism.

Vice-President Henry A. Wallace is today the outstanding heir of the Populists. He fights against monopoly, but at the same time he opposes socialism as the enemy of free enterprise. He is nostalgic for the kind of freedom which flourished in the earlier stages of capitalist development. Free individual enterprise was then definitely a historically progressive force, promoting the quest for labor-saving devices and increasing the productivity of human labor. But rooted in this type of free competition, and growing out of it as inevitably as night follows day, have been the vast units of industrial production and the aggregations of private capital which the Populists have opposed.

Looking backward and trying to restore the past is futile, if not positively harmful to human progress. Today our problem is concerned with utilizing the enormous technical advance, the intricate economic structure built up under capitalist development. Life itself poses the question: How can this complex social mechanism be brought into the service of the people as a whole? How can its vast productive capacity be addressed to the abolition of poverty? Can we find a richer freedom in working together, using together this great apparatus of production and distribution?

Advocates of socialism have always believed that the piling up of private wealth (with its relative impoverishment of the masses) and the undue control of our economic and political life by an inner circle of finance capitalists are inherent in the private ownership of socially utilized means of production. Only through social ownership, instead of private ownership, can the immensely valuable mechanism of industry and trade be brought into the service of the people as a whole. Only thus can political freedom and equality become a reality in our complex society.

This is so clear and so obvious that those who fear any advance toward socialism spend much thought and energy on misrepresenting the one country which now operates under a socialist economy. Valiant devotion of the Soviet people to their socialist motherland has begun to dispel the fog of prejudice. But most Americans—including Vice-President Wallace—do not yet understand the reality of popular democratic rule in the Soviet Union.

The political structure of Soviet democracy differs from our kind of democratic structure, but this does not mean that it denies to any of the people the full participation in political life which democracy implies. And the national planning of their socialist economy has not ruled out the "freedom of enterprise" which some Americans set up as a fetish to be defended against "socialist regimentation." For in the Soviet Union it is supremely true that its miracles of economic development have been produced by the free initiative of the people themselves. They have resulted from a constant interplay of individual effort, local planning, and free popular government on the one hand, and nationwide consultation, nationwide planning, and expert assistance on the other.

Furthermore, like our own United States, the Soviet Union has been a pioneer among nations. From our American Revolution there developed the first democratic republic. From the Russian Revolution of 1917 there developed the first nation which has shaped its economy to assure to all citizens freedom from want.

Populism in the United States was rooted primarily among farmers and other small producers and traders—classes which had dominated economic life until they were oppressed and displaced by the growth of industry.

Socialism has its mass base primarily among the industrial wage workers, a class brought forth by capitalist development and destined for a greater role as capitalism gives place to socialism. Workers are being shaped by life itself for creative effort, creative leadership toward socialism. Working together, jobless together, organizing for better conditions and realizing together that they are producing wealth for the capitalist class—wage-workers learn from experience to see more clearly than any other class the meaning of solidarity. Their common struggles lay the foundation for a socialist freedom far richer than any individual freedom of business competition.

Standing with the workers are many idealists from other economic groups, together with working farmers, salaried technicians, and others who feel the pressure of the capitalist system and know that only by moving together toward new horizons can we create a better world.

The man who initiated the attack on the standard interpretation of Populism is RICHARD HOFSTADTER (b. 1916), DeWitt Clinton Professor of History at Columbia University, where he completed his graduate studies. An internationally respected scholar and author of *Social Darwinism in American Thought* (1944), *The American Political Tradition* (1948), and other works, he has gained wide acclaim for his thought-provoking writings. He feels that scholars have been too prone to emphasize constructive features of Populism. The following selection from his Pulitzer prize-winning *The Age of Reform* (1955) pinpoints the negative phases of Populism, which he believes have been ignored. It has had special appeal to those who have been skeptical of the liberal phases of agrariansim. *

Richard Hofstadter

The Folklore of Populism

There is indeed much that is good and usable in our Populist past. While the Populist tradition had defects that have been too much neglected, it does not follow that the virtues claimed for it are all fictitious. Populism was the first modern political movement of practical importance in the United States to insist that the federal government has some responsibility for the common weal; indeed, it was the first such movement to attack seriously the problems created by industrialism. The complaints and demands and prophetic denunciations of the Populists stirred the latent liberalism in many Americans and startled many conservatives into a new flexibility. Most of the "radical" reforms in the Populist program proved in later years to be either harmless or useful. In at least one important area of American life a few Populist leaders in the South attempted something profoundly radical and humane— to build a popular movement that would cut across the old barriers of race—until persistent use of the Negro bogy distracted their following. To discuss the broad ideology of the Populist does them some injustice, for it was in their concrete programs that they added most constructively to our political life, and in their more general picture of the world that they were most credulous and vulnerable. Moreover, any account of the fallibility of Populist thinking that does not ack-

* From *The Age of Reform*, by Richard Hofstadter. © Copyright 1955 by Richard Hofstadter. Reprinted by permission of Alfred A. Knopf, Inc. Pp. 61–67, 70–71, 74–83, 86–89, 91–93.

nowledge the stress and suffering out of which that thinking emerged will be seriously remiss. But anyone who enlarges our portrait of the Populist tradition is likely to bring out some unseen blemishes. In the books that have been written about the Populist movement, only passing mention has been made of its significant provincialism; little has been said of its relations with nativism and nationalism; nothing has been said of its tincture of anti-Semitism.

The Populist impulse expressed itself in a set of notions that represent what I have called the "soft" side of agrarianism. These notions, which appeared with regularity in the political literature, must be examined if we are to re-create for ourselves the Populist spirit. To extract them from the full context of the polemical writings in which they appeared is undoubtedly to oversimplify them; even to name them in any language that comes readily to the historian of ideas is perhaps to suggest that they had a formality and coherence that in reality they clearly lacked. But since it is less feasible to have no labels than to have somewhat too facile ones, we may enumerate the dominant themes in Populist ideology as these: the idea of a golden age; the concept of natural harmonies; the dualistic version of social struggles; the conspiracy theory of history; and the doctrine of the primacy of money. The last of these I will touch upon in connection with the free-silver issue. Here I propose to analyze the others, and to show how they were nurtured by the traditions of the agrarian myth.

The utopia of the Populists was in the past, not the future. According to the agrarian myth, the health of the state was proportionate to the degree to which it was dominated by the agricultural class, and this assumption pointed to the superiority of an earlier age. The Populists looked backward with longing to the lost agrarian Eden, to the republican America of the early years of the

nineteenth century in which there were few millionaires and, as they saw it, no beggars, when the laborer had excellent prospects and the farmer had abundance, when statesmen still responded to the mood of the people and there was no such thing as the money power.[1] What they meant—though they did not express themselves in such terms—was that they would like to restore the conditions prevailing before the development of industrialism and the commercialization of agriculture. It should not be surprising that they inherited the traditions of Jacksonian democracy, that they revived the old Jacksonian cry: "Equal Rights for All, Special Privileges for None," or that most of the slogans of 1896 echoed the battle cries of 1836.[2] General James B. Weaver, the Populist candidate for the presidency in 1892, was an old Democrat and Free-Soiler, born during the days of Jackson's battle with the United States Bank, who drifted into the Greenback movement after a short spell as a Republican, and from there to Populism. His book, *A Call to Action*, published in 1892, drew up an indictment of the business corporation which reads like a Jacksonian polemic. Even in those hopeful early days of the People's Party, Weaver projected no grandiose plans for the future, but lamented the course of recent history, the growth of economic oppression, and the emergence of great contrasts of wealth and poverty, and called upon his readers to do "All in [their] power to arrest the alarming tendencies of our times."[3]

Nature, as the agrarian tradition had it, was beneficent. The United States was abundantly endowed with rich land and rich resources, and the "natural" consequence of such an endowment should be the prosperity of the people. If the people failed to enjoy prosperity, it must be because of a harsh and arbitrary intrusion of human greed and error. "Hard times, then," said one popular writer, "as well as the bankruptcies, enforced idleness, starvation, and the crime, misery, and moral degradation growing out of conditions like the present, being unnatural, not in accordance with, or the result of any natural law, must be attributed to that kind of unwise and pernicious legislation which history proves to have produced similar results in all ages of the world. It is the mission of the age to correct these errors in human legislation, to adopt and establish policies and systems, in accord with, rather than in opposition to divine law."[4] In assuming a lush natural order whose workings were being deranged by human laws, Populist writers were again drawing on the Jacksonian tradition, whose spokesmen also had pleaded for a proper obedience to "natural" laws as a prerequisite of social justice.[5]

Somewhat akin to the notion of the beneficence of nature was the idea of a natural harmony of interests among the productive classes. To the Populist mind there was no fundamental conflict between the farmer and the worker, between the toiling people and the small businessman. While there might be corrupt individuals in any group, the underlying interests of the productive majority were the same; predatory behavior existed only because it was initiated and underwritten by a small parasitic minority in the highest places of power. As opposed to the idea that society consists of a number of different and frequently clashing interests—the social pluralism expressed, for instance, by Madison in the *Federalist*—the Populists adhered, less formally to be sure, but quite persistently, to a kind of social dualism: although they knew perfectly well that society was composed of a number of classes, for all practical purposes only one simple division need be considered. There were two nations. "It is a struggle," said Sockless Jerry Simpson, "between the robbers and the robbed."[6] "There are but two sides in the conflict that is being waged in this country today," declared a Populist manifesto. "on the one side are the allied hosts of monopolies,

the money power, great trusts and railroad corporations, who seek the enactment of laws to benefit them and impoverish the people. On the other are the farmers, laborers, merchants, and all other poeple who produce wealth and bear the burdens of taxation. . . . Between these two there is no middle ground."[7] "On the one side," said Bryan in his famous speech against the repeal of the Sherman Silver Purchase Act, "stand the corporate interests of the United States, the moneyed interests, aggregated wealth and capital, imperious, arrogant, compassionless. . . . On the other side stand an unnumbered throng, those who gave to the Democratic party a name and for whom it has assumed to speak."[8] The people versus the interests, the public versus the plutocrats, the toiling multitude versus the money power—in various phrases this central antagonism was expressed. From this simple social classification it seemed to follow that once the techniques of misleading the people were exposed, victory over the money power ought to be easily accomplished, for in sheer numbers the people were overwhelming. "There is no power on earth that can defeat us," said General Weaver during the optimistic days of the campaign of 1892. "It is a fight between labor and capital, and labor is in the vast majority."[9]

The problems that faced the Populists assumed a delusive simplicity: the victory over injustice, the solution for all social ills, was concentrated in the crusade against a single, relatively small but immensely strong interest, the money power. "With the destruction of the money power," said Senator Peffer, "the death knell of gambling in grain and other commodities will be sounded; for the business of the worst men on earth will have been broken up, and the mainstay of the gamblers removed. It will be an easy matter, after the greater spoilsmen have been shorn of their power, to clip the wings of the little ones. Once get rid of the men who hold the country by the throat, the parasites can be easily removed."[10] Since the old political parties were the primary means by which the people were kept wandering in the wilderness, the People's Party advocates insisted, only a new and independent political party could do this essential job.[11] As the silver question became more prominent and the idea of a third party faded, the need for a monolithic solution became transmuted into another form: there was only one *issue* upon which the money power could really be beaten and this was the money issue. "When we have restored the money of the Constitution," said Bryan in his Cross of Gold speech, "all other necessary reforms will be possible; but . . . until this is done there is no other reform that can be accomplished."

While the conditions of victory were thus made to appear simple, they did not always appear easy, and it would be misleading to imply that the tone of Populistic thinking was uniformly optimistic. Often, indeed, a deep-lying vein of anxiety showed through. The very sharpness of the struggle, as the Populists experienced it, the alleged absence of compromise solutions and of intermediate groups in the body politic, the brutality and desperation that were imputed to the plutocracy—all these suggested that failure of the people to win the final contest peacefully could result only in a total victory for the plutocrats and total extinction of democratic institutions, possibly after a period of bloodshed and anarchy. "We are nearing a serious crisis," declared Weaver. "If the present strained relations between wealth owners and wealth producers continue much longer they will ripen into frightful disaster. This universal discontent must be quickly interpreted and its causes removed."[12] "We meet," said the Populist platform of 1892, "in the midst of a nation brought to the verge of moral, political, and material ruin. Corruption dominates the ballot-box, the Legislatures, the Congress, and touches even the ermine of the

bench. The people are demoralized. . . . The newspapers are largely subsidized or muzzled, public opinion silenced, business prostrated, homes covered with mortgages, labor impoverished, and the land concentrating in the hands of the capitalists. The urban workmen are denied the right to organize for self-protection, imported pauperized labor beats down their wages, a hireling standing army, unrecognized by our laws, is established to shoot them down, and they are rapidly degenerating into European conditions. The fruits of the toil of millions are boldly stolen to build up colossal fortunes for a few, unprecedented in the history of mankind; and the possessors of these, in turn, despise the Republic and endanger liberty." Such conditions foreboded "the destruction of civilization, or the establishment of an absolute despotism." . . .

There was something about the Populist imagination that loved the secret plot and the conspiratorial meeting. There was in fact a widespread Populist idea that all American history since the Civil War could be understood as a sustained conspiracy of the international money power.

The pervasiveness of this way of looking at things may be attributed to the common feeling that farmers and workers were not simply oppressed but oppressed deliberately, consciously, continuously, and with wanton malice by "the interests." It would of course be misleading to imply that the Populists stand alone in thinking of the events of their time as the results of a conspiracy. This kind of thinking frequently occurs when political and social antagonisms are sharp. Certain audiences are especially susceptible to it—particularly, I believe, those who have attained only a low level of education, whose access to information is poor,[13] and who are so completely shut out from access to the centers of power that they feel themselves completely deprived of self-defense and subjected to unlimited manipulation by those who wield power. There are, moreover, certain types of popular movements of dissent that offer special opportunities to agitators with paranoid tendencies, who are able to make a vocational asset out of their psychic disturbances.[14] Such persons have an opportunity to impose their own style of thought upon the movements they lead. It would of course be misleading to imply that there are no such things as conspiracies in history. . . .

The financial argument behind the conspiracy theory was simple enough. Those who owned bonds wanted to be paid not in a common currency but in gold, which was at a premium; those who lived by lending money wanted as high a premium as possible to be put on their commodity by increasing its scarcity. The panics, depressions, and bankruptcies caused by their policies only added to their wealth; such catastrophes offered opportunities to engross the wealth of others through business consolidations and foreclosures. Hence the interests actually relished and encouraged hard times. The Greenbackers had long since popularized this argument, insisting that an adequate legal-tender currency would break the monopoly of the "Shylocks." Their demand for $50 of circulating medium per capita, still in the air when the People's Party arose, was rapidly replaced by the less "radical" demand for free coinage of silver. But what both the Greenbackers and free-silverites held in common was the idea that the contraction of currency was a deliberate squeeze, the result of a long-range plot of the "Anglo-American Gold Trust." Wherever one turns in the Populist literature of the nineties one can find this conspiracy theory expressed. It is in the Populist newspapers, the proceedings of the silver conventions, the immense pamphlet literature broadcast by the American Bimetallic League, the Congressional debates over money; it is elaborated in such popular books as Mrs. S. E. V. Emery's *Seven Financial Conspiracies Which Have Enslaved the*

American People or Gordon Clark's *Shylock: as Banker, Bondholder, Corruptionist, Conspirator.*

Mrs. Emery's book, first published in 1887, and dedicated to "the enslaved people of a dying republic," achieved great circulation, especially among the Kansas Populists. According to Mrs. Emery, the United States had been an economic Garden of Eden in the period before the Civil War. The fall of man had dated from the war itself, when "the money kings of Wall Street" determined that they could take advantage of the wartime necessities of their fellow men by manipulating the currency. "Controlling it, they could inflate or depress the business of the country at pleasure, they could send the warm life current through the channels of trade dispensing peace, happiness, and prosperity, or they could check its flow, and completely paralyze the industries of the country."[15] With this great power for good in their hands, the Wall Street men preferred to do evil. Lincoln's war policy of issuing greenbacks presented them with the dire threat of an adequate supply of currency. So the Shylocks gathered in convention and "perfected" a conspiracy to create a demand for their gold.[16] The remainder of the book was a recital of a series of seven measures passed between 1862 and 1875 which were alleged to be a part of this continuing conspiracy, the total effect of which was to contract the currency of the country further and further until finally it squeezed the industry of the country like a hoop of steel.[17]. . .

"Coin" Harvey, the author of the most popular single document of the whole currency controversy, *Coin's Financial School*, also published a novel, *A Tale of Two Nations*, in which the conspiracy theory of history was incorporated into a melodramatic tale. In this story the powerful English banker Baron Rothe plans to bring about the demonetization of silver in the United States, in part for his own aggrandizement but also to prevent the power of the United States from outstripping that of England. He persuades an American Senator (probably John Sherman, the *bête noire* of the silverites) to cooperate in using British gold in a campaign against silver. To be sure that the work is successful, he also sends to the United States a relative and ally, one Rogasner, who stalks through the story like the villains in the plays of Dion Boucicault, muttering to himself such remarks as "I am here to destroy the United States—Cornwallis could not have done more. For the wrongs and insults, for the glory of my own country, I will bury the knife deep into the heart of this nation."[18] Against the plausibly drawn background of the corruption of the Grant administration, Rogasner proceeds to buy up the American Congress and suborn American professors of economics to testify for gold. He also falls in love with a proud American beauty, but his designs on her are foiled because she loves a handsome young silver Congressman from Nebraska who bears a striking resemblance to William Jennings Bryan!

One feature of the Populist conspiracy theory that has been generally overlooked is its frequent link with a kind of rhetorical anti-Semitism. The slight current of anti-Semitism that existed in the United States before the 1890's had been associated with problems of money and credit.[19] During the closing years of the century it grew noticeably.[20] While the jocose and rather heavy-handed anti-Semitism that can be found in Henry Adams's letters of the 1890's shows that this prejudice existed outside Populist literature, it was chiefly Populist writers who expressed that identification of the Jew with the usurer and the "international gold ring" which was the central theme of the American anti-Semitism of the age. The omnipresent symbol of Shylock can hardly be taken in itself as evidence of anti-Semitism, but the frequent references to the House of Rothschild make it clear that for many silverites the Jew was an

organic part of the conspiracy theory of history. Coin Harvey's Baron Rothe was clearly meant to be Rothschild; his Rogasner (Ernest Seyd?) was a dark figure out of the coarsest anti-Semitic tradition. "You are very wise in your way," Rogasner is told at the climax of the tale, "the commercial way, inbred through generations. The politic, scheming, devious way, inbred through generations also."[21] One of the cartoons in the effectively illustrated *Coin's Financial School* showed a map of the world dominated by the tentacles of an octopus at the site of the British Isles, labeled: "Rothschilds."[22] In Populist demonology, anti-Semitism and Anglophobia went hand in hand.

The note of anti-Semitism was often sounded openly in the campaign for silver. A representative of the New Jersey Grange, for instance, did not hesitate to warn the members of the Second National Silver Convention of 1892 to watch out for political candidates who represented "Wall Street, and the Jews of Europe."[23] Mary E. Lease described Grover Cleveland as "the agent of Jewish bankers and British gold."[24] Donnelly represented the leader of the governing Council of plutocrats in *Caesar's Column*, one Prince Cabano, as a powerful Jew, born Jacob Isaacs; one of the triumvirate who lead the Brotherhood of Destruction is also an exiled Russian Jew, who flees from the apocalyptic carnage with a hundred million dollars which he intends to use to "revive the ancient splendors of the Jewish race, in the midst of the ruins of the world."[25] One of the more elaborate documents of the conspiracy school traced the power of the Rothschilds over America to a transaction between Hugh McCulloch, Secretary of the Treasury under Lincoln and Johnson, and Baron James Rothschild. "The most direful part of this business between Rothschild and the United States Treasury was not the loss of money, even by hundreds of millions. It was the resignation of the country itself INTO THE HANDS

OF ENGLAND, as England had long been resigned into the hands of HER JEWS."[26]

Such rhetoric, which became common currency in the movement, later passed beyond Populism into the larger stream of political protest. By the time the campaign of 1896 arrived, an Associated Press reporter noticed as "one of the striking things" about the Populist convention at St. Louis "the extraordinary hatred of the Jewish race. It is not possible to go into any hotel in the city without hearing the most bitter denunciation of the Jews as a class and of the particular Jews who happen to have prospered in the world."[27] This report may have been somewhat overdone, but the identification of the silver cause with anti-Semitism did become close enough for Bryan to have to pause in the midst of his campaign to explain to the Jewish Democrats of Chicago that in denouncing the policies of the Rothschilds he and his silver friends were "not attacking a race; we are attacking greed and avarice which know no race or religion."[28]

It would be easy to misstate the character of Populist anti-Semitism or to exaggerate its intensity. For Populist anti-Semitism was entirely verbal. It was a mode of expression, a rhetorical style, not a tactic or a program. It did not lead to exclusion laws, much less to riots or pogroms. There were, after all, relatively few Jews in the United States in the late 1880's and early 1890's, most of them remote from the areas of Populist strength. It is one thing, however, to say that this prejudice did not go beyond a certain symbolic usage, quite another to say that a people's choice of symbols is of no significance. Populist anti-Semitism does have its importance—chiefly as a symptom of a certain ominous credulity in the Populist mind. It is not too much to say that the Greenback-Populist tradition activated most of what we have of modern popular anti-Semitism in the United States.[29] From Thaddeus Stevens and Coin Harvey to Father Coughlin, and from Brooks and Henry Adams to Ezra Pound, there has been a curiously persistent linkage between anti-Semitism and money and credit obsessions. A full history of modern anti-Semitism in the United States would reveal, I believe, its substantial Populist lineage, but it may be sufficient to point out here that neither the informal connection between Bryan and the Klan in the twenties nor Thomas E. Watson's conduct in the Leo Frank case were altogether fortuitous.[30] And Henry Ford's notorious anti-Semitism of the 1920's, along with his hatred of "Wall Street," were the foibles of a Michigan farm boy who had been liberally exposed to Populist notions.[31]

The conspiratorial theory and the associated Anglophobic and Judophobic feelings were part of a larger complex of fear and suspicion of the stranger that haunted, and still tragically haunts, the nativist American mind. This feeling, though hardly confined to Populists and Bryanites, was none the less exhibited by them in a particularly virulent form. Everyone remote and alien was distrusted and hated—even Americans, if they happened to be city people. The old agrarian conception of the city as the home of moral corruption reached a new pitch. Chicago was bad; New York, which housed the Wall Street bankers, was farther away and worse; London was still farther away and still worse. This traditional distrust grew stronger as the cities grew larger, and as they were filled with immigrant aliens. As early as 1885 the Kansas preacher Josiah Strong had published *Our Country*, a book widely read in the West, in which the cities were discussed as a great problem of the future, much as though they were some kind of monstrous malignant growths on the body politic.[32] Hamlin Garland recalled that when he first visited Chicago, in the late 1880's, having never seen a town larger than Rockford, Illinois, he naturally assumed that it swarmed with thieves. "If the city is miles across," he wondered, "how am I to get from the railway station to my hotel without being assaulted?" While such extreme fears could be quieted by some contact with the city, others were actually confirmed—especially when the farmers were confronted with city prices.[33] Nativist prejudices were equally aroused by immigration, for which urban manufacturers, with their insatiable demand for labor, were blamed. "We have become the world's melting pot," wrote Thomas E. Watson. "The scum of creation has been dumped on us. Some of our principal cities are more foreign than American. The most dangerous and corrupting hordes of the Old World have invaded us. The vice and crime which they have planted in our midst are sickening and terrifying. What brought these Goths and Vandals to our shores? The manufacturers are mainly to blame. They wanted cheap labor: and they didn't care a curse how much harm to our future might be the consequence of their heartless policy.[34]. . .

The Populists distinguished between wars for humanity and wars of conquest. The first of these they considered legitimate, but naturally they had difficulty in discriminating between the two, and they were quite ready to be ballyhooed into a righteous war, as the Cuban situation was to show. During the early nineteenth century popular sentiment in the United States, especially within the democratic camp, had been strong for the republican movements in Europe and Latin America. With the coming of the nineties and the great revulsion against the outside world, the emphasis was somewhat changed; where sympathy with oppressed and revolutionary peoples had been the dominant sentiment in the past, the dominant sentiment now seemed rather to be hatred of their governments. That there must always be such an opposition between peoples and governments the Populist mind did not like to question, and even the most democratic governments of Europe were persistently looked upon as though they were nothing but reactionary monarchies.[35]. . .

It is no coincidence, then, that Populism and jingoism grew concurrently in the United States during the 1890's. The rising mood of intolerant nationalism was a nationwide thing, certainly not confined to the regions of Populist strength; but among no stratum of the population was it stronger than among the Populists. Moreover it was on jingoist issues that the Populist and Bryanite sections of the country, with the aid of the yellow press and mány political leaders, achieved that rapport with the masses of the cities which they never succeeded in getting on economic issues. Even conservative politicians sensed that, whatever other grounds of harmony were lacking between themselves and the populace of the hinterland, grounds for unity could be found in war.

The first, and for the Populists the preferred, enemy would have been England, the center of the gold power. *Coin's Financial School* closed with a better philippic against England: "If it is claimed we must adopt for our money the metal England selects, and can have no independent choice in the matter, let us make the test and find out if it is true. It is not American to give up without trying. If it is true, let us attach England to the United States and blot her name out from among the nations of the earth. A war with England would be the most popular ever waged on the face of the earth. . .the most just war ever waged by man."[36] Some leaders of the Republican Party, which had attempted to appease the powerful silver sentiment in 1890 by passing the Sherman Silver Purchase Act, made a strategic move in the troubled year of 1894 to capture Western sentiment. On May 2 there opened in London an unofficial bimetallic conference in which American bimetallists were represented by Brooks Adams and Senator Wolcott of Colorado; fifteen prominent Senators, including outstanding Republicans, cabled their endorsement of international bimetallism. Senator Lodge proposed in the Senate to blackmail Britain by passing a discriminatory tariff against her if she did not consent to a bimetallic plan, a scheme nicely calculated to hold in line some of the Western silverite jingoes and Anglophobes.[37]. . .

As we review these aspects of Populist emotion, an odd parallel obtrudes itself. Where else in American thought during this period do we find this militancy and nationalism, these apocalyptic forebodings and drafts of world-political strategies, this hatred of big businessmen, bankers, and trusts, these fears of immigrants and urban workmen, even this occasional toying with anti-Semitic rhetoric? We find them, curiously enough, most conspicuous among a group of men who are in all obvious respects the antithesis of the Populists. During the late 1880's and the '90's there emerged in the eastern United States a small imperialist elite representing, in general, the same type that had once been Mugwumps, whose spokesmen were such solid and respectable gentlemen as Henry and Brooks Adams, Theodore Roosevelt, Henry Cabot Lodge, John Hay, and Albert J. Beveridge. While the silverites were raging openly and earnestly against the bankers and the Jews, Brooks and Henry Adams were expressing in their sardonic and morosely cynical private correspondence the same feelings, and acknowledging with bemused irony their kinship at this point with the mob. While Populist Congressmen and newspapers called for war with England or Spain, Roosevelt and Lodge did the same, and while Mrs. Lease projected her grandiose schemes of world partition and tropical colonization, men like Roosevelt, Lodge, Beveridge, and Mahan projected more realistic plans for the conquest of markets and the annexation of territory. While Populist readers were pondering over Donnelly's apocalyptic fantasies, Brooks and Henry Adams were also bemoaning the approaching end of their

type of civilization, and even the characteristically optimistic T. R. could share at moments in "Brooks Adams' gloomiest anticipations of our gold-ridden, capitalist-bestridden, usurer-mastered future." Not long after Mrs. Lease wrote that "we need a Napoleon in the industrial world who, by agitation and education, will lead the people to a realizing sense of their condition and the remedies,"[38] Roosevelt and Brooks Adams talked about the threat of the eight-hour movement and the danger that the country would be "enslaved" by the organizers of the trusts, and played with the idea that Roosevelt might eventually lead "some great outburst of the emotional classes which should at least temporarily crush the Economic Man."[39]

Not only were the gentlemen of this imperialist elite better read and better fed than the Populists, but they despised them. This strange convergence of unlike social elements on similar ideas has its explanation, I believe, in this: both the imperialist elite and the Populists had been bypassed and humiliated by the advance of industrialism, and both were rebelling against the domination of the country by industrial and financial capitalists. The gentlemen wanted the power and status they felt due them, which had been taken away from their class and type by the *arriviste* manufacturers and railroaders and the all-too-potent banking houses. The Populists wanted a restoration of agrarian profits and popular government. Both elements found themselves impotent and deprived in an industrial culture and balked by a common enemy. On innumerable matters they disagreed, but both were strongly nationalistic, and amid the despairs and anxieties of the nineties both became ready for war if that would unseat or even embarrass the moneyed powers, or better still if it would topple the established political structure and open new opportunities for the leaders of disinherited farmers or for ambitious gentlemen. But if there seems to be in this situation any suggestion of a forerunner or analogue of modern authoritarian movements, it should by no means be exaggerated. The age was more innocent and more fortunate than ours, and by comparison with the grimmer realities of the twentieth century many of the events of the nineties take on a comic-opera quality. What came in the end was only a small war and a quick victory; when the farmers and the gentlemen finally did coalesce in politics, they produced only the genial reforms of Progressivism; and the man on the white horse turned out to be just a graduate of the Harvard boxing squad, equipped with an immense bag of platitudes, and quite willing to play the democratic game.

---

[1] Thomas E. Watson: *The Life and Times of Andrew Jackson* (Thomson, Ga., 1912), p. 325: "All the histories and all the statesmen agree that during the first half-century of our national existence, we had no poor. A pauper class was unthought of: a beggar, or a tramp never seen." Cf. Mrs. S. E. V. Emery: *Seven Financial Conspiracies Which Have Enslaved the American People* (Lansing, ed. 1896), pp. 10–11.

[2] Note for instance the affectionate treatment of Jacksonian ideas in Watson, op. cit., pp. 343–4.

[3] James B. Weaver: *A Call to Action* (Des Moines, 1892), pp. 377–8.

[4] B. S. Heath: *Labor and Finance Revolution* (Chicago, 1892), p. 5.

[5] For this strain in Jacksonian thought, see Richard Hofstadter: "William Leggett, Spokesman of Jacksonian Democracy," *Political Science Quarterly*, Vol. XLVIII (December 1943), pp. 581–94, and *The American Political Tradition*, pp. 60–1.

[6] Elizabeth N. Barr: "The Populist Uprising," in William E. Connelley, ed.: *A Standard History of Kansas and Kansans*, Vol. II, p. 1170.

[7] Ray Allen Billington: *Westward Expansion* (New York, 1949), p. 741.

[8] Allan Nevins: *Grover Cleveland* (New York, 1933), p. 540; Heath, op. cit., p. 27: "The world has always contained two classes of people, one that lived by honest labor and the other that lived off of honest labor." Cf. Governor Lewelling of Kansas: "Two great forces are forming in battle line: the same under different form and guise that have long been in deadly antagonism, represented in master and slave, lord and vassal, king and peasant, despot and serf, landlord and tenant, lender and borrower, organized avarice and the necessities of the divided and helpless poor." James A. Barnes: *John G. Carlisle* (New York, 1931), pp. 254–5.

[9] George H. Knoles: *The Presidential Campaign and Election of 1892* (Stanford, 1942), p. 179.

[10] William A. Peffer: *The Farmer's Side* (New York, 1891), p. 273.

[11] Ibid., pp. 148–50.

[12] Weaver, op. cit., p. 5.

[13] In this respect it is worth pointing out that in later years, when facilities for realistic exposure became more adequate, popular attacks on "the money power" showed fewer elements of fantasy and more of reality.

[14] See, for instance, the remarks about a mysterious series of international assassinations with which Mary E. Lease opens her book *The Problem of Civilization Solved* (Chicago, 1895).

[15] Emery, op. cit., p. 13.

[16] Ibid., pp. 14–18.

[17] The measures were: the "exception clause" of 1862; the National Bank Act of 1863; the retirement of the greenbacks, beginning in 1866; the "credit-strengthening act" of March 18, 1869; the refunding of the national debt in 1870; the demonetization of silver in 1873; and the destruction of fractional paper currency in 1875.

[18] W. H. Harvey: *A Tale of Two Nations* (Chicago, 1894), p. 69.

[19] Anti-Semitism as a kind of rhetorical flourish seems to have had a long underground history in the United States. During the panic of 1837, when many states defaulted on their obligations, many of which were held by foreigners, we find Governor McNutt of Mississippi defending the practice by baiting Baron Rothschild: "The blood of Judas and Shylock flows in his veins, and he unites the qualities of both his countrymen. . . ." Quoted by George W. Edwards: *The Evolution of Finance Capitalism* (New York, 1938), p. 149. Similarly we find Thaddeus Stevens assailing "the Rothschilds, Goldsmiths, and other large money dealers" during his early appeals for greenbacks. See James A. Woodburn: *The Life of Thaddeus Stevens* (Indianapolis, 1913), pp. 576, 579.

[20] See Oscar Handlin: "American Views of the Jew at the Opening of the Twentieth Century," *Publications of the American Jewish Historical Society*, no. 40 (June 1951), pp. 323–44.

[21] Harvey: *A Tale of Two Nations*, p. 289; cf. also p. 265: "Did not our ancestors . . . take whatever women of whatever race most pleased their fancy?"

[22] Harvey: *Coin's Financial School* (Chicago, 1894), p. 124; for a notable polemic against the Jews, see James B. Goode: *The Modern Banker* (Chicago, 1896), chapter xii.

[23] *Proceedings of the Second National Silver Convention* (Washington, 1892), p. 48.

[24] Mary E. Lease: *The Problem of Civilization Solved*, pp. 319–20; cf. p. 291.

[25] Donnelly, op. cit., pp. 147, 172, 331.

[26] Gordon Clark, *Shylock: as Banker, Bondholder, Corruptionist, Conspirator* (Washington, 1894), pp. 59–60; for the linkage between anti-Semitism and the conspiracy theme, see pp. 2, 4, 8, 39, 55–8, 102–3, 112–13, 117. There was a somewhat self-conscious and apologetic note in populistic anti-Semitism. Remarking that "the aristocracy of the world is now almost al-

together of Hebrew origin," one of Donnelly's characters explains that the terrible persecutions to which the Jews had been subjected for centuries heightened the selective process among them, leaving "only the strong of body, the cunning of brain, the longheaded, the persistent . . . and now the Christian world is paying, in tears and blood, for the sufferings inflicted by their bigoted and ignorant ancestors upon a noble race. When the time came for liberty and fair play the Jew was master in the contest with the Gentile, who hated and feared him." *Caesar's Column*, p. 37. In another fanciful tale Donnelly made amends to the Jews by restoring Palestine to them and making it very prosperous. *The Golden Bottle* (New York and St. Paul, 1892), pp. 280–1.

[27] Quoted by Edward Flower: *Anti-Semitism in the Free Silver and Populist Movements and the Election of 1896*, unpublished M.A. thesis, Columbia University, 1952, p. 27; this essay is illuminating on the development of anti-Semitism in this period and on the reaction of some of the Jewish press.

[28] William Jennings Bryan: *The First Battle* (Chicago, 1897), p. 581.

[29] I distinguish here between popular anti-Semitism, which is linked with political issues, and upper-class anti-Semitism, which is a variety of snobbery. It is characteristic of the indulgence which Populism has received on this count that Carey McWilliams in his *A Mask for Privilege: Anti-Semitism in America* (Boston, 1948) deals with early American anti-Semitism simply as an upper-class phenomenon. In his historical account of the rise of anti-Semitism he does not mention the Greenback-Populist tradition. Daniel Bell: "The Grass Roots of American Jew Hatred," *Jewish Frontier*, Vol. XI (June 1944), pp. 15–20, is one of the few writers who has perceived that there is any relation between latter-day anti-Semites and the earlier Populist tradition. See also Handlin, op. cit. Arnold Rose has pointed out that much of American anti-Semitism is intimately linked to the agrarian myth and to resentment of the ascendancy of the city. The Jew is made a symbol of both capitalism and urbanism, which are themselves too abstract to be satisfactory objects of animosity. *Commentary*, Vol. VI (October 1948), pp. 374–78.

[30] For the latter see Woodward: *Tom Watson*, chapter xxiii.

[31] Keith Sward: *The Legend of Henry Ford* (New York, 1948), pp. 83–4, 113–14, 119–20, 132, 143–60. Cf. especially pp. 145–6: "Ford could fuse the theory of Populism and the practice of capitalism easily enough for the reason that what he carried forward from the old platforms of agrarian revolt, in the main, were the planks

that were most innocent and least radical. Like many a greenbacker of an earlier day, the publisher of the Dearborn *Independent* was haunted by the will-o'-the-wisp of 'money' and the bogy of 'race.' It was these superstitions that lay at the very marrow of his political thinking." For further illustration of the effects of the Populist tradition on a Mountain State Senator, see Oscar Handlin's astute remarks on Senator Pat McCarran in "The Immigration Fight Has Only Begun," *Commentary*, Vol. XIV (July 1952), pp. 3–4.

[32] Josiah Strong: *Our Country* (New York, 1885), chapter x; for the impact of the city, see Arthur M. Schlesinger: *The Rise of the City* (New York, 1933).

[33] Hamlin Garland: *A Son of the Middle Border* (New York, ed. 1923), pp. 269, 295.

[34] Watson: *Andrew Jackson*, p. 326; cf. *Caesar's Column*, p. 131: "The silly ancestors of the Americans called it 'national development' when they imported millions of foreigners to take up the public lands and left nothing for their own children."

[35] See Harvey's *Coin on Money, Trusts, and Imperialism, passim.*

[36] *Coin's Financial School*, pp. 131–2.

[37] Nevins, op. cit., pp. 608–9.

[38] Lease, op. cit., p. 7. Thomas E. Watson wrote in 1902 a lengthy biography: *Napoleon, a Sketch of His Life, Character, Struggles, and Achievements*, in which Napoleon, "the moneyless lad from despised Corsica, who stormed the high places of the world, and by his own colossal strength of character, genius, and industry took them," is calmly described as "the great Democratic despot." Elsewhere Watson wrote: "There is not a railway king of the present day, not a single self-made man who has risen from the ranks to become chief in the vast movement of capital and labor, who will not recognize in Napoleon traits of his own character; the same unflagging purpose, tireless persistence, silent plotting, pitiless rush to victory . . ."—which caused Watson's biographer to ask what a Populist was doing celebrating the virtues of railway kings and erecting an image of capitalist acquisitiveness for his people to worship. "Could it be that the Israelites worshipped the same gods as the Philistines? Could it be that the only quarrel between the two camps was over a singular disparity in the favors won?" Woodward, op. cit., pp. 340–2.

[39] Matthew Josephson: *The President Makers* (New York, 1940), p. 98. See the first three chapters of Josephson's volume for a penetrating account of the imperialist elite. Daniel Aaron has an illuminating analysis of Brooks Adams in his *Men of Good Hope* (New York, 1951).

Another scholar joining the attack on the standard interpretation of Populism is VICTOR C. FERKISS (b. 1925), a political scientist who teaches at Georgetown University. A native of New York City, he was educated at the University of California, Berkeley, Yale, and the University of Chicago, where he obtained his Ph.D. in 1954. The following article is based largely on his doctoral dissertation, which was written during the McCarthy era. The positive tone of the essay appealed to students who sought new explanations for past happenings. He maintains that Populism was a negative force in the advancement of democracy, and focuses attention on issues that Hofstadter failed to discuss. *

Victor C. Ferkiss

Populist Influences
on American Fascism

The doctrinal roots of American fascist thought have long remained obscure for reasons inherent in recent American history itself. Essentially fascist popular movements grew up in America during the period 1929–41 at a time when American publicists and intellectuals were rediscovering America in their reaction to the growth of fascism and nazism abroad. Increased regard for American tradition among hitherto alienated intellectuals made them reluctant to admit that movements such as those led by Huey Long, Father Coughlin, and Gerald L. K. Smith were not the result of temporary psychological aberrations on the part of the masses but were, instead, the culmination of an ideological development stemming from such generally revered movements as Populism and "agrarian democracy." For them fascism was by definition un-American. . . .

Any search for the roots of American fascism must necessarily be preceded by a clear understanding of the essential features of the movement. Few definitions of fascism are without their ardent supporters and violent detractors. Because of space limitations, the definition used herein can only be explicated, not defended.

We hold that the essential elements of fascism in the American context are:

---

* From Victor C. Ferkiss, "Populist Influences in American Fascism," *The Western Political Quarterly*, X (June, 1957), 350–367, 372–373. Reprinted by permission of the University of Utah, copyright owners. Footnotes omitted.

(1) An economic program designed to appeal to a middle class composed largely of farmers and small merchants which feels itself being crushed between big business—and especially big finance—on the one hand, and an industrial working class which tends to question the necessity of the wage system and even of private property itself on the other. Such an economic program will include violent attacks against big business and finance—particularly the latter—and will advocate their control by the government in the interest of the farmer and small merchant.

(2) Nationalism. International co-operation is held to be a device by means of which supranational conspirators are able to destroy the freedom and well-being of the people. A desire to stay aloof from foreign affairs is the American (and English) fascist substitute for imperialism, and any imperialistic venture undertaken by either of these countries will ordinarily be denounced as a conspiracy engineered by selfish economic interests. . . .

(3) A despair of liberal democratic institutions, resulting from the belief that the press and the other communication media have been captured by the enemy, as have the two major political parties. Political power is held to belong to the people as a whole and is considered to be best exercised through some form of plebiscitary democracy. Leaders with a popular mandate will sweep aside any procedural obstacles to the fulfillment of the popular will, and will purge those institutions which stand in the way of the instantaneous attainment of popular desires. . . .

(4) An interpretation of history in which the causal factor is the machinations of international financiers. The American Revolution, the fight of Jackson against the bank, and Lincoln's war against the South and its British allies are all considered episodes in the struggle of the people against the "money power." International finance is held responsible for the "crime of '73," entry into World War I, and the 1929 Depression. Communism is the creation of international finance and a system in which the money power strips off the mask of sham democracy and rules nakedly. A Communist state naturally results when the concentration of economic power in the hands of a few members of the international conspiracy reaches its logical terminus. . . .

How this creed, on which all the segments of the American fascist movement were in basic agreement, arose logically from the Populist creed, and how the American fascist leaders attracted substantially the same social groups and sectional interests as had Populism is the burden of this paper.

The Populist Message

Populism is used herein as a generic term to denote not merely the People's party, or Populism properly so-called, but such closely allied movements as the Greenback party, the Bryan free silver crusades, La Follette Progressivism, and similar manifestations of primarily agrarian revolt against domination by Eastern financial and industrial interests.

The Populist economic program was, of course, tailored to the needs of the farmers of the prairies. The class struggle throughout American history has traditionally been waged not by laborers against employers, but by debtors against creditors. Agrarian discontent had a long history prior to the Civil War. Following that conflict the West was opened to settlers under the Homestead Act. These settlers needed money for capital and were dependent upon the railroads to sell their goods. The value of money appreciated so greatly that they had difficulty in paying their debts. The railroads, controlled by Eastern financial interests, were able to exploit them. The local governments and press were to a considerable extent the creatures of

Eastern money, as were most of the local banks. A struggle began for a government which would regulate credit and control the railroads so that the settlers might prosper as middle-class landowners. This struggle reached its climax in Bryan's campaign of 1896 and abated thereafter as a result of the increasing amount of gold in circulation.

Economic program. The motives of these Populists were similar to those which produced the rank-and-file twentieth-century American fascist. The Populists' aim was not the destruction of capitalism as they knew it, but was rather its preservation and extension. They were interested in protecting capitalism and the small entrepreneur from abuse at the hands of the monopolist and the banker. Populism was a middle-class movement; the Populists saw in Eastern finance capitalism a force which, unless controlled, would destroy their status and reduce them to proletarians.

The Populist economic program centered about the need for public control of credit. Senator Peffer of Kansas described the Populist economic creed in the following words:

If there is any part of the Populist's creed which he regards as more important than another, and which, therefore, may be taken as leading, it is that which demands the issue and circulation of national money, made by authority of the people for their use, money that they will at any and all times be responsible for, money that persons in business can procure on good security at cost, money handled only by public agencies, thus doing away with all back issues of paper to be used as money.[1]

... This, then, was the most important plank in the Populist economic platform— the restoration to the people of their "sovereign power" to control money; private control is held to be a violation of the Consti-

tution and a usurpation of a governmental function. In addition, the railroads and similar interests must also be controlled by a strong, central government capable of crushing the selfish few in the interests of the nation as a whole.

Populists believe in the exercise of national authority in any and every case where the general welfare will be promoted thereby. ...

Populism teaches the doctrine that the rights and interests of the whole body of the people are superior, and, therefore, paramount to those of individuals. The Populist believes in calling in the power of the people in every case where the public interest requires it or will be promoted.[2]

Public power will protect the national interest against the selfish few. ...

Nationalism and anti-Semitism. Nationalism was to be found in Populism principally in the form of a suspicious isolationism which regarded foreign involvements as inimical to the national interest and as existing solely to promote the interests of Eastern capitalists. Economic nationalism was reflected in Peter Cooper's proposal for protective tariffs, and Populists often advocated severe restrictions on immigration. ...

The final ingredient of Populist nationalism was the anti-Semitism endemic throughout the rural West. The correlation between hatred of Jews (though in a mild form and wholly without dialectical formulation) with sentiment for Bryan has been noted by Professor Oscar Handlin. The prairie farmer associated the Jew with the merchant, the financier, and the corrupt and domineering Eastern city.

Populist racial hostility was directed against those believed capable of destroying the small farmer's economic status and way of life. To the Midwesterner, the Negro presented no problem since he was not physically

---

[1] At Des Moines, Iowa, August 18, 1897; quoted in "Populism, Its Rise and Fall" by Senator Peffer, *Chicago Daily Tribune,* July 7, 1899, p. 12.

[2] Senator Peffer, *op. cit.*

present and since he (unlike the Jew) could hardly be pictured as scheming to undermine the position of Midwestern farmers and shopkeepers from afar. In the South, the situation was more complex. At first white and Negro farmers stood together in a common economic struggle against "the interests." However, it was not too long before the xenophobic feelings to which Populist orators appealed in their attempts to arouse the "red-necks'" opposition to the interests endangered this small-farmer solidarity. Hatred of the different could focus on the black skin of the Negro as well as on the uncalloused hands of the white plantation owner, and the enemies of Populism were not tardy about taking advantage of this fact to divide their foes. . . .

Plebiscitary democracy. Populism's predisposition to anti-Semitism and to nationalism and its suspicion of the corruption of urban life are all tendencies opposed to those trends which issue in democratic socialism in the humanist tradition; these proclivities more closely coincide with the patterns of conservative or fascist social beliefs. There is a tendency on the part of observers to overlook the true import of these propensities because of the role played by Populist and Progressive movements in the development of American democracy. To these movements America largely owes, for better or for worse, the direct primary, popular election of senators, the initiative, the referendum and recall, and the Wisconsin tradition of clean, efficient government, conducted with the assistance of experts.

Yet some qualifications must be made of the popular conception of Populism as a democratic or liberal force. First, the agrarian trend toward political reform was rarely based upon any broad ideas about human freedom or the fuller human life. Populist-inspired reforms were instrumental. The farmer wanted particular political changes because he felt they were needed to effect the defeat of the "money power" and to gain for farmers certain direct economic benefits. From their support of these measures we cannot infer a willingness on the part of the Populists to support egalitarian measures which would conduce to the benefit of others with different substantive aims.

Secondly, all these reforms serve to strengthen not liberalism but direct, plebiscitary democracy. They are designed to make the will of the majority immediately effective and to sweep away intervening institutions such as the legislatures, the older political parties, and the courts, which have all been corrupted by the money power. . . .

In short, Populist political thought is compatible in spirit with the plebiscitary democracy of a Huey Long or a Hitler. This is not to say that Populists and Progressives universally opposed free speech as such or that Weaver, Lindbergh, Sr., or the elder La Follette would ever have seized power and then denied to the opposition an opportunity to regain power through constitutional means. They did believe that the opposition, including the press, was corrupt and antisocial; but they still believed that an aroused people could regain control of the government from the selfish few who had usurped it. . . .

The Degeneration of Populism

The degeneration of Populism into incipient fascism can be explained by the rebuffs and defections it suffered during the early years of the twentieth century. These reverses and the resulting fragmentation of its constituency meant the periodic peeling away of its more liberal elements. The Populist creed aroused no interest in serious American intellectual circles. . . .

At the turn of the century the Populists were already unhappy about the failure of organized labor to support the Bryan crusade. The alleged betrayal of the Populists by Theodore Roosevelt widened the political rift between the Westerners and urban reformism. The Populists accused Roosevelt of waging a sham battle against finance and of having cruelly deceived La Follette regarding the 1912 presidential nomination. The resulting split drained from Populism many internationalists and humanists, who thereupon cast their lot permanently with the urban liberal movement, leaving the Populist forces even more regional and agrarian than they had previously been. . . .

Illustrative of the condition in which Populism now found itself is the history of the North Dakota Non-Partisan League, a radical farmers organization favoring state banking and state handling of crop storage. The League was founded in 1915 by Arthur C. Townley, a Socialist, and William Lemke, a young lawyer who while still in college had said, "if I can find out what people hate most I can build a new political party around it." The hatred Lemke found was hatred of European capitalism and of the "war-party" in Washington and New York, and on this base the League was built. The League was widely opposed as seditious, and organizers were sometimes run out of town by patriotic mobs. Nonetheless, the League flourished. It dominated political life in North Dakota for many years and was influential in the politics of neighboring states as well.

In the House of Representatives, the fight against Wilson's foreign policy was led by the most radical of the Populist survivors, Charles A. Lindbergh, Sr., of Minnesota. Lindbergh did much to synthesize the Populist interpretation of history. In his speeches and books he traced the machinations of the "money-power" back as far as the Civil War, pointed up their responsibility for "internationalism," and portrayed them as leading the nation into World War I to protect Britain, head of the international financial trust. This thesis was not generally popular and the double-barreled charge of economic radicalism and treachery was leveled against it.

Other Populists suffered physical violence for speaking out against internationalism. Ernest Lundeen, later a Farmer-Labor senator from Minnesota and a close associate of Nazi agents, was driven out of a Minnesota town in a locked refrigerator car as a result of his denunciation of the League of Nations.

But Populism survived this persecution. Its effect was mainly to strengthen the alliance between nationalistic isolationism and hatred of finance capitalism, the Eastern urban liberals, and the press. Belated revenge was enjoyed by the Populists when, in 1934, Senator Gerald Nye of North Dakota (a product of Non-Partisan League politics and a former associate of the French biological elitist Alexis Carrel in a plan to institute a guild system in the United States) headed a Senate committee which proved to the satisfaction of many that financial and industrial interests dragged nations into wars for the sake of larger profits.

A last attempt at uniting the Populist holdouts and the Eastern urban liberals was made in 1924, when, in conjunction with the Socialist party and the American Federation of Labor, the Progressive party ran a ticket composed of Bob La Follette for President and Burton K. Wheeler (Democratic senator from Montana) for Vice-President. The ticket received slightly less than five million votes, largely in the Middle and Far West, but the dissatisfaction which produced this ticket was soon swallowed up in the wave of normalcy.

The Emergence of American Fascism

. . . It is as difficult to pinpoint the essence of fascist doctrine as it is to supply a satisfactory one-sentence definition of Populism, and the history of the American fascist movement, with its shifting personal and electoral alliances, is at least as complex as that of Populism. There is, however, a remarkably coherent common core of doctrine uniting such widely divergent intellectuals as the economist Lawrence Dennis and the poet Ezra Pound; and fascism as a popular movement, from its emergence under Senator Long and Father Coughlin in 1930 to its demise under Gerald L. K. Smith in 1946, was united by a common conception of what constituted the principal problems and in what direction a solution to them ought to be sought. . . .

Economic program. The American fascist economic program, like that of Populism, advocates the use of strong governmental controls in a few key areas in order to protect a middle class of independent farmers and shopkeepers from becoming impoverished proletarians as a result of the "boom and bust" business cycle which, it is maintained, is engineered by the Eastern bankers for their own enrichment. But fascism's program was designed to appeal not merely to the rural interests but also to those members of the urban lower-middle class (especially the white-collar workers) who were unwilling to identify themselves with organized labor and feared its power almost as much as they feared that of big business.

The program is again based on a mono-causal interpretation of economic problems which makes it possible to apply simple, once-and-for-all solutions. For Huey Long the solution is a demagogic Share-Our-Wealth program, designed to make "Every Man a King" through the redistribution of wealth and the prevention of its concentration in the hands of the few by means of restrictions on big business. Most fascists have chosen the old Populist remedy—control of the monetary supply so as to stabilize the ratio between goods and prices and to destroy the usury of private banking which, it is held, is the source of the concentration of economic power.

Populist economics is revived *in toto* by the fascists, and the claim is openly made that the fascists are the inheritors of the Populist mantle. The core of the fascist program is ex-

emplified in the Nye-Sweeney bill (H.R. 6382) introduced in Congress in 1935 at the behest of Father Coughlin. Its purpose as stated in its preamble was:

. . . To restore to Congress its constitutional power to issue money and regulate the value thereof; to provide for the orderly distribution of the abundance with which a beneficent Creator has blessed us; to establish and maintain the purchasing power of money at fixed and equitable levels; to increase the prices of agricultural products to a point where they will yield the cost of production plus a fair profit to the farmer; to provide a living and just annual wage which will enable every citizen willing to work and capable of working to maintain and educate his family on an increasing level or standard of living; to repay debts with dollars of equal value; to lift in part the burden of taxation; and for other purposes.

Monetary manipulation is still (as it was for Bryan) the sovereign remedy.

Save for Dennis and Coughlin, American fascists generally offered money reform as the sole economic plank in their program for social reform, since for them it was the issue on which all other economic reforms hinged. This concentration on monetary reform fostered the fascist view that capitalism and communism are basically similar in that both concentrate all economic power in the hands of a few. For the fascist the evils of capitalism and communism can be avoided only through the creation of a strong state. The state will then be able to intervene to save private property from becoming concentrated in the hands of the few through social control of those economic mechanisms which are used by the usurious international bankers to destroy their economic competitors and to control both the nation's economy and its government. . . .

Nationalism and anti-Semitism. American fascist nationalism is also of a piece with the nationalism of the Populists. Save for Dennis' desire to make American influence felt in Latin America, where he had served in the Foreign Service, imperialism is no part of

American fascist doctrine. The emphasis is upon the material and moral superiority of America. She needs a strong defense but should remain aloof from foreign quarrels. Nationalism takes the form of doctrinaire isolationism in which the Populist monetary interpretation of history is used to explain current international problems and to indicate their proper solution. Thus World War II is held to be simply a plot on the part of the Wall Street–London group of international bankers to use the common people of the Western nations to defeat the revolt against banker domination being led by Italy and Germany. . . .

Dennis was active in holding that the fascist powers should be allowed to win their battle against dying capitalist democracy and that America should not interfere. Long, had he lived, would doubtless have continued to be as ardently isolationist as he had been when he claimed that the League of Nations was controlled by "the European enemies of this country." Save for the emotional nationalistic rallies of Smith's Christian Nationalist party, American fascists vented their nationalism in a negative manner, attacking the Western democracies, seeking to keep America out of World War II, and proclaiming all internationalist movements, from Union Now to communism, to be fronts for the international bankers and world Jewry.

While the only anti-Negro agitation in the American fascist movement is to be found in Smith's later period and not at all in the other major fascist ideologues, anti-Semitism is rampant. The Jew is branded a national enemy and is identified with the banker, the communist, and the anti-nationalist. Alleged Jewish racial solidarity is claimed to be not merely a link that reinforces the economic ties of international finance, but one which binds such seemingly disparate but actually compatible groups as the international capitalists and the communists in common cause against the American nation and people. This anti-Semitic agitation ranges from Dennis' remarks distinguishing between Americans and "Jews living in America" to the paranoic diatribes of Pound, although save for Pound and a few street agitators like McWilliams, all the important American fascists denied they were anti-Semitic, just as they denied they were fascist. Thus another Populist predilection was resurrected in a more violent form—the identification of Jews, New York, and international finance. To this, fascism added the identification of all three with communism. . . .

Plebiscitary democracy. The American fascist ideal of plebiscitary democracy was best exemplified by Huey Long, who used the mandate given to him by the voters as an excuse to create a rubber-stamp legislature, pack the courts, and attempt to intimidate the press. Said Long:

> Down in Louisiana we have no dictatorship, but what I call a closer response to the will of the people. It is a government of initiative and referendum. We called a convention to amend the Constitution, and when these amendments were approved by the people, we merely called the legislature together to pass enabling acts. Everything that has been done in Louisiana is merely to carry out the will of the people as expressed in the amendments to the constitution. That's not a dictatorship.
>
> They [the legislature] look to somebody to get up the program for them; they're committed to the general program and so we get through with it without squandering the State's time and money.

. . . The old Populist theme that liberal institutions and the party system are the tools of the rich is now echoed by people who, unlike the early Populists, have despaired of capturing or reforming them. The use of force to ensure the triumph of the popular will, which in the Populist era meant the employment of mob violence to prevent sheriffs' sales of mortgaged property, will in the new dispensation be the prerogative primarily of various storm troop and youth movements such as those developed by Smith and Coughlin.

Political action. The influence of Populism in the generation of American fascism can be illustrated by political as well as by intellectual similarities. A high degree of correlation has been shown to exist between the vote given La Follette in 1924 and Lemke in 1936 and the counties which withdrew their support from the Democratic party in 1940 because of opposition to its foreign policy but returned to the fold in 1948. Samuel Lubell has stressed the importance of the Germanic ethnic origin of the populations of these areas and concludes that their support of Populist candidates in the past was the result primarily of isolationist and pro-German sympathies rather than of their economic beliefs. . . .

The death of Huey Long in 1935 deprived American fascism of its most politically eligible candidate; Father Coughlin's National Union for Social Justice collapsed after the defeat of Lemke; and under the spur of war preparations economic conditions were improving. Fascist leaders had to search for new issues and new political figures with which to make their bid for power. Nationalism was to be the dominant issue, but the development of anti-Semitism and an increased emphasis on foreign policy did not mean that Populist economic doctrine was to be ignored or replaced and Populist historical theory was to prove useful in providing a rationale for isolationism.

Many monetary reform advocates like ex-Senator Owen and Professor Soddy maintained their connections with the fascist movement and augmented its strength and dynamism, and most fascist leaders could be numbered among the supporters of "money-reform." Symbolically, Jacob Coxey, the old Populist veteran, in 1939 told a gathering that Hitler was doing the world a service by ridding Germany and Europe of the power of usury.

But the big issue of the moment was foreign policy. The controversy over intervention in World War II gave the native fascists an issue on which to seek popular support and political power. The America First Committee provided the culture in which the seeds of American fascism were to grow. . . .

The Future of American Fascism

The war years dealt a blow to the forces of Populism and fascism from which (unlike the situation after World War I) recovery seems unlikely. Senators Wheeler, Nye and the late Rush Holt were defeated at the polls and have been unable to regain office. Langer still survives: he was one of three senators to vote against ratification of the United Nations Charter (the other two were the old Progressive Hiram Johnson and the former Farmer-Laborite Henrik Shipstead). But Langer is now only a quaint individualist rather than a spokesman for a social and political movement.

Sympathetic interest in the ideology of Populism is at a low point. Liberal Progressive historians like Hesseltine still may complain that Franklin Roosevelt did not solve the banking problem; nonetheless, Roosevelt did so complicate the situation by dividing fiscal functions between the Federal Reserve and the Treasury that it would be well-nigh impossible to make the problem of credit control a clear-cut political issue. The great apostles of monetary reform are dead politically, and soft versus hard money has subsided into merely one of many policy differences between Republicans and Democrats, one element in the problem of how to adjust the dials in a controlled economy.

The farmers have decided that their need is not fundamental reform of the system, but that log-rolling for price supports will do, and they have been absorbed into the great push-and-pull of America's quasi-syndicalist economy. Despite price fluctuations the

"Farm Bloc" is now mainly a "have" group, even in the states of the Middle Border.

The urban adherents of such leaders as Father Coughlin are now also largely numbered among the "haves" and are little interested in schemes for social reform. In recent years they constituted an important segment of the following of Senator Joseph McCarthy, a man who employed many of the same general tactics as their former leaders but who lacked their racial and economic programs. Some surviving fascist leaders such as Gerald L. K. Smith now devote most of their time to agitating against the United Nations. Others concentrate on such peripheral targets as UNESCO and progressive education. Most of those who figured in the fascist movements of the thirties, however, have melted into the mainstream of the contemporary "radical right."

The American fascist movement dissolved because the radical right appropriated its demagogic nationalism and anticommunism and because its Populist-inspired economic panaceas lost their relevance and appeal as a result of changes in the conditions of American life. For these reasons it seems unlikely that American fascism will ever again be able to attract a substantial popular following.

Among the first to answer the revisionist charges was C. VANN WOODWARD (b. 1908), Sterling Professor of History at Yale University, one of the foremost living historians of the South. A native of Arkansas, he is author of several well-received books, including *Tom Watson* (1938), *Origins of the New South* (1951), and *The Burden of Southern History* (1960). In the following article he surveys the revisionist position in a moderate and judicious manner. He is critical of those who would seek to repudiate our Populist heritage. *

C. Vann Woodward

The Populist Heritage
and the Intellectual

During the long era of the new deal one had little difficulty living in comparative congeniality with the Populist heritage. The two periods had much in common, and it was easy to exaggerate their similarities and natural to seek antecedents and analogies in the earlier era. Because of the common setting of severe depression and economic dislocation, Populism seemed even closer to the New Deal than did Progressivism, which had a setting of prosperity. Common to both Populists and New Dealers was an antagonism to the values of the dominant leaders of the business community bordering on alienation. They shared a sense of urgency and an edge of desperation about the demand for reform. And in both, so

far as the South and West were concerned, agricultural problems were the most desperate, and agrarian reforms occupied the center of attention. It seemed entirely fitting that Hugo Black of Alabama and Harry Truman of Missouri—politicians whose political style and heritage were strongly Populistic—should lead New Deal reform battles. From many points of view the New Deal was neo-Populism.

The neo-Populism of the present bred a Populistic view of the past. American historiography of the 1930's and 1940's reflects a strong persuasion of this sort. The most popular college textbook in American history was written by a Midwesterner who was

*From C. Vann Woodward, "The Populist Heritage and the Intellectual," *The American Scholar*, LIX (Winter, 1959–1960), 55–72. Footnotes omitted.

friendly to Populism and was himself the foremost historian of the movement. The leading competitor among textbooks shared many of the Populist leanings, even though one of its authors was a Harvard patrician and the other a Columbia urbanite. A remarkably heterogeneous assortment struck up congenial ties in the neo-Populist coalition. Small-town Southerners and big-city Northerners, Texas mavericks and Hudson River aristocrats, Chapel Hill liberals and Nashville agrarians were all able to discover some sort of identity in the heritage. The South rediscovered ties with the West, the farmer with labor. The New York–Virginia axis was revived. Jacksonians were found to have urban affiliations and origins. Not to be outdone, the Communists staked out claims to selected Populist heroes.

Many intellectuals made themselves at home in the neo-Populist coalition and embraced the Populist heritage. They had prepared the way for affiliation in the twenties when they broke with the genteel tradition, adopted the mucker pose, and decided that conventional politics and the two major parties were the province of the boobocracy and that professional politicians were clowns or hypocrites. In the thirties intellectuals made naïve identification with farmers and workers and supported their spokesmen with enthusiasm. The Populist affinity outlasted the New Deal, survived the war, and perhaps found its fullest expression in the spirit of indulgent affection with which intellectuals often supported Harry Truman and his administration.

Hardly had Truman left the White House, however, when the Populist identification fell into disgrace and intellectuals began to repudiate the heritage. "Populist" suddenly became a term of opprobrium, in some circles a pejorative epithet. This resulted from no transfer of affection to Truman's successor, for there was very little of that among intellectuals. It resulted instead from the shock of the encounter with McCarthyism. Liberals and intellectuals bore the brunt of the degrading McCarthyite assault upon standards of decency. They were rightly alarmed and felt themselves betrayed. Something had gone badly wrong. They were the victims of a perversion of the democracy they cherished, a seamy and sinister side of democracy to which they now guiltily realized they had all along tended to turn a blind or indulgent eye. Stung by consciousness of their own negligence or naïveté, they reacted with a healthy impulse to make up for lost time and to confront their problem boldly with all the critical resources at their command. The consequence has been a formidable and often valuable corpus of social criticism.

Not one of the critics, not even the most conservative, is prepared to repudiate democracy. There is general agreement that the fault lay in some abuse or perversion of democracy, and was not inherent in democracy itself. All the critics are aware that these abuses and perversions had historic antecedents and had appeared in various guises and with disturbing frequency in national history. These unhappy tendencies are variously described as "mobism," "direct democracy," or "plebiscitarianism," but there is a surprising and apparently spontaneous consensus of preference for "Populism." Although the word is usually capitalized, most of the critics do not limit its reference to the political party that gave currency to the term. While there is general agreement that the essential characteristics designated by the term are best illustrated by an agrarian movement in the last decade of the nineteenth century, some of the critics take the liberty of applying it to movements as early as the Jacksonians, or earlier, and to twentieth-century phenomena as well.

The reasons for this convergence from several angles upon "Populism" as the appropriate designation for an abhorred abuse are not all clear. A few, however, suggest themselves. Populism is generally thought of as an entirely Western affair, Wisconsin as a seedbed of the movement, and Old Bob La Follette as a foremost exponent. None of these assumptions is historically warranted, but it is true that Senator McCarthy came from Wisconsin, that much of his support came from the Middle West, and that there are some similarities between the two movements. The impression of similarity has been enhanced by the historical echo of their own alarm that modern intellectuals have caught in the rather hysterical fright with which Eastern conservatives reacted to Populism in the nineties.

This essay is not concerned with the validity of recent analysis of the "radical right" and its fascistic manifestations in America. It is concerned only with the tendency to identify Populism with these movements and with the implied rejection of the Populist tradition. It is admittedly very difficult, without risk of misrepresentation and injustice, to generalize about the way in which numerous critics have employed the Populist identification. They differ widely in the meaning they attribute to the term and the importance they attach to the identification. Among the critics are sociologists, political scientists, poets and journalists, as well as historians, and there is naturally a diversity in the degree of historical awareness and competence they command. Among points of view represented are the New Conservative, the New Liberal, the liberal-progressive, the Jewish, the Anglophile, and the urban, with some overlapping. There are no conscious spokesmen of the West or the South, but some are more-or-less conscious representatives of the urban East. Every effort will be made not to attribute to one the views of another.

Certain concessions are due at the outset. Any fair-minded historian will acknowledge the validity of some of the points scored by the new critics against the Populist tradition and its defenses. It is undoubtedly true that liberal intellectuals have in the past constructed a flattering image of Populism. They have per-

mitted their sympathy with oppressed groups to blind them to the delusions, myths and foibles of the people with whom they sympathized. Sharing certain political and economic doctrines and certain indignations with the Populists, they have attributed to them other values, tastes and principles that the Populists did not actually profess. It was understandably distasteful to dwell upon the irrational or retrograde traits of people who deserved one's sympathy and shared some of one's views. For undertaking this neglected and distasteful task in the spirit of civility and forbearance which, for example, Richard Hofstadter has shown, some of the new critics deserve much credit. All of them concede some measure of value in the Populist heritage, although none so handsomely as Hofstadter, who assumes that Populism and Progressivism are strongly enough established in our tradition to withstand criticism. Others are prone to make their concessions more perfunctory and to hasten on with the job of heaping upon Populism, as upon a historical scapegoat, all the ills to which democracy is heir.

The danger is that under the concentrated impact of the new criticism the risk is incurred not only of blurring a historical image but of swapping an old stereotype for a new one. The old one sometimes approached the formulation that Populism is the root of all good in democracy, while the new one sometimes suggests that Populism is the root of all evil. Uncritical repetition and occasional exaggeration of the strictures of some of the critics threaten to result in establishing a new maxim in American political thought: *Radix malorum est Populismus.*

Few of the critics engaged in the reassessment of Populism and the analysis of the New American Right would perhaps go quite so far as Peter Viereck, when he writes, "Beneath the sane economic demands of the Populists of 1880-1900 seethed a mania of xenophobia, Jew-baiting, intellectual-baiting, and thought-controlling lynch-spirit."

Yet this far from exhausts the list of unhappy or repulsive aberrations of the American spirit that have been attributed to Populism. Other aberrations are not pictured as a "seething mania" by any one critic, but by one or another the Populists are charged with some degree of responsibility for Anglophobia, Negrophobia, isolationism, imperialism, jingoism, paranoidal conspiracy-hunting, anti-Constitutionalism, anti-intellectualism, and the assault upon the right of privacy, among others. The Populist virus is seen as no respecter of the barriers of time or nationality. According to Edward A. Shils, "populism has many faces. Nazi dictatorship had markedly populistic features. . . . Bolshevism has a strand of populism in it too. . . ." And there was among fellow travelers a "populistic predisposition to Stalinism." On the domestic scene the strand of populistic tradition "is so powerful that it influences reactionaries like McCarthy and left-wing radicals and great upperclass personalities like Franklin Roosevelt." And according to Viereck, populistic attitudes once "underlay Robespierre's Committee of Public Safety" and later "our neo-Populist Committee on un-American Activities."

Among certain of the critics there is no hesitancy in finding a direct continuity between the nineteenth-century Populists and twentieth-century American fascism and McCarthyism. Victor C. Ferkiss states flatly that "American fascism has its roots in American populism. It pursued the same ends and even used many of the same slogans. Both despaired of achieving a just society under the joined banners of liberalism and capitalism." His assertion supports Viereck's suggestion that "Since the same impulses and resentments inspire the old Populism and the new nationalist right, let us adopt 'neo-Populism' as the proper term for the latter group." Talcott Parsons believes that "The elements of continuity between Western agrarian populism and McCarthyism are not by any means purely fortuitous," and Edward Shils

thinks the two are connected by "a straight line." It remained for Viereck to fill in the gap: "The missing link between the Populism of 1880-1900 and the neo-Populism of today—the missing link between Ignatius Donnelly and the McCarthy movement—was Father Charles Coughlin."

There is a strong tendency among the critics not only to identify Populism and the New Radical Right, but to identify both with certain regions, the West and South, and particularly the Middle West. "The areas which produced the populism of the end of the nineteenth century and the early twentieth century have continued to produce them," writes Shils. Viereck puts it somewhat more colorfully: "The Bible-belt of Fundamentalism in religion mostly overlapped with the farm-belt of the Populist, Greenback, and other free-silver parties in politics. Both belts were anti-intellectual, anti-aristocratic, anti-capitalist." Talcott Parsons and Ferkiss likewise stress the regional identity of Populist-Radical Right ideology, and Viereck supplies an interesting illustration: "Out of the western Populist movement came such apostles of thought-control and racist bigotry as Tom Watson. . . ."

If so many undesirable traits are conveniently concentrated along geographical lines, it might serve a useful purpose to straighten out the political geography of Populism a bit. In the first place, as Hofstadter and other historians of the movement have noted, Populism had negligible appeal in the Middle Western states, and so did the quasi-Populism of William Jennings Bryan. Wisconsin, Minnesota, Iowa, Illinois and states east of them went down the line for McKinley, Hanna, gold and the Old Conservatism (and so did Old Bob La Follette). Only in the plains states of the Dakotas, Nebraska and Kansas were there strong Populist leanings, and only they and the mountain states went for Bryan in 1896. At the crest of the Populist wave in 1894 only Nebraska polled a Populist vote comparable in strength to that run up in Alabama, Georgia and North Carolina.

For the dubious distinction of being the leading Populist section, the South is in fact a strong contender; and if the test is merely quasi-Populism, the pre-eminence of the former Confederacy is unchallengeable. It was easily the most solidly Bryan section of the country, and its dogged loyalty far outlasted that of the Nebraskan's native state. But a more important test was third-party Populism, the genuine article. The remarkable strength the Populists manifested in the Lower South was gained against far more formidable obstacles than any ever encountered in the West. For there they daily faced the implacable dogmas of racism, white solidarity, white supremacy and the bloody shirt. There was indeed plenty of "thought control and racist bigotry and lynch-spirit," but the Populists were far more often the victims than the perpetrators. They had to contend regularly with foreclosure of mortgages, discharge from jobs, eviction as tenants, exclusion from church, withholding of credit, boycott, social ostracism and the endlessly reiterated charge of racial disloyalty and sectional disloyalty. Suspicion of loyalty was in fact *the* major psychological problem of the Southern Populists, as much so perhaps as the problem of loyalty faced by radicals of today. They contended also against cynical use of fraud comparable with any used against Reconstruction, methods that included stuffed ballot boxes, packed courts, packed registration and election boards, and open bribery. They saw election after election stolen from them and heard their opponents boast of the theft. They were victims of mobs and lynchers. Some fifteen Negroes and several white men were killed in the Georgia Populist campaign of 1892, and it was rare that a major election in the Lower South came off without casualties.

Having waged their revolt at such great cost, the Southern Populists were far less willing to compromise their principles than were their Western brethren. It was the Western Populists who planned and led the movement to sell out the party to the silverites, and the Southern Populists who fought and resisted the drift to quasi-Populism. The Southerners were consistently more radical, more insistent upon their economic reforms, and more stubbornly unwilling to lose their party identity in the watered-down populism of Bryan than were Western Populists.

There is some lack of understanding about *who* the Southern Populists were for and against, as well as *what* they were for and against. Edward Shils writes that the "economic and political feebleness and pretensions to breeding and culture" of the "older aristocratic ruling class" in the South provided "a fertile ground for populistic denunciation of the upper classes." Actually the Southern Populists directed their rebellion against the newer ruling class, the industrialists and businessmen of the New South instead of the old planters. A few of the quasi-Populists like Ben Tillman did divert resentment to aristocrats like Wade Hampton. But the South was still a more deferential society than the rest of the country, and the Populists were as ready as the railroads and insurance companies to borrow the prestige and name of a great family. The names of the Populist officals in Virginia sounded like a roll call of colonial assemblies or Revolutionary founding fathers: Page, Cocke, Harrison, Beverley, Ruffin. There were none more aristocratic in the Old Dominion. General Robert E. Lee, after the surrender at Appomattox, retired to the ancestral home of Edmund Randolph Cocke after his labors. His host was later Populist candidate for governor of the state. As the editor of their leading paper, the allegedly Anglophobic Populists of Virginia chose Charles H. Pierson, an ordained Anglican priest, English by birth, Cambridge graduate and theological student of Oxford. To be sure, the Populist leaders of Virginia were not typical of the movement in the South. But neither were Jefferson, Madison, Monroe and John Taylor typical of *their* movement in the South: there were never enough aristocrats to go around. Some states had to make do with cruder customers as leaders in both Jeffersonian and Populist movements, and in the states to the west there doubtless was less habitual dependence on aristocrats even if they had been more readily available.

In their analysis of the radical right of modern America, the new critics have made use of the concept of "status resentment" as the political motivation of their subjects. They distinguish between "class politics," which has to do with the correction of economic deprivations, and "status politics," which has no definite solutions and no clear-cut legislative program but responds to irrational appeals and vents aggression and resentment for status insecurity upon scape-goats—usually ethnic minorities. Seymour Martin Lipset, who appears at times to include Populism in the category, has outlined the conditions typical of periods when status politics become ascendant. These are, he writes, "periods of prosperity, especially when full employment is accompanied by inflation, and when many individuals are able to improve their economic position." But the conditions under which Populism rose were exactly the opposite. severe depression, critical unemployment and crippling currency contraction, when few were able to improve their economic position—and certainly not farmers in cash-crop staple agriculture.

The Populists may have been bitten by status anxieties, but if so they were certainly not bred of upward social mobility, and probably few by downward mobility either—for the simple reason that there was not much further downward for most Populists to go, and had not been for some time. Populism was hardly "status politics," and I should hesitate to call it "class politics." It was more nearly "interest politics," and more specifically "agricultural interest politics."

Whatever concern the farmers might have had for their status was overwhelmed by desperate and immediate economic anxieties. Not only their anxieties but their proposed solutions and remedies were economic. While their legislative program may have been often naïve and inadequate, it was almost obsessively economic and, as political platforms go, little more irrational than the run of the mill.

Yet one of the most serious charges leveled against the Populists in the reassessment by the new critics is an addiction to just the sort of irrational obsession that is typical of status politics. This is the charge of anti-Semitism. It has been documented most fully by Richard Hofstadter and Oscar Handlin and advanced less critically by others. The prejudice is attributed to characteristic Populist traits—rural provinciality, and ominous credulity and an obsessive fascination with conspiracy. Baffled by the complexities of monetary and banking problems, Populist ideologues simplified them into a rural melodrama with Jewish international bankers as the principal villains. Numerous writings of Western Populists are cited that illustrate the tendency to use Jewish financiers and their race as scapegoats for agrarian resentment. Hofstadter points out that Populist anti-Semitism was entirely verbal and rhetorical and cautions that it can easily be misconstrued and exaggerated. Nevertheless, he is of the opinion "that the Greenback-Populist tradition activated most of what we have of modern popular anti-Semitism in the United States."

In the voluminous literature of the nineties on currency and monetary problems—problems that were much more stressed by silverites and quasi-Populists than by radical Populists—three symbols were repetitively used for the plutocratic adversary. One was institutional, Wall Street; and two were ethnic, the British and Jewish bankers. Wall Street was by far the most popular and has remained so ever since among politicians of agrarian and Populistic tradition. Populist agitators used the ethnic symbols more or less indiscriminately, British along with Jewish, although some of them bore down with peculiar viciousness on the Semitic symbol. As the new critics have pointed out, certain Eastern intellectuals of the patrician sort, such as Henry and Brooks Adams and Henry Cabot Lodge, shared the Populist suspicion and disdain of the plutocracy and likewise shared their rhetorical anti-Semitism. John Higham has called attention to a third anti-Semitic group of the nineties, the poorer classes in urban centers. Their prejudice cannot be described as merely verbal and rhetorical. Populists were not responsible for a protest signed by fourteen Jewish societies in 1899 that "No Jew can go on the street without exposing himself to the danger of being pitilessly beaten." That was in Brooklyn. And the mob of 1902 that injured some two hundred people, mostly Jewish, went into action in Lower East Side New York.

Populist anti-Semitism is not to be excused on the ground that it was verbal, nor dismissed because the prejudice received more violent expression in urban quarters. But all would admit that the charge of anti-Semitism has taken on an infinitely more ominous and hideous significance since the Nazi genocide furnaces than it ever had before, at least in Anglo-American society. The Populists' use of the Shylock symbol was not wholly innocent, but they used it as a folk stereotype, and little had happened in the Anglo-Saxon community between the time of Shakespeare and that of the Populists that burdened the latter with additional guilt in repeating the stereotype.

The South, again, was a special instance. Much had happened there to enhance the guilt of racist propaganda and to exacerbate racism. But anti-Semitism was not the trouble, and to stress it in connection with the South of the nineties would be comparable to stressing anti-Negro feeling in the Arab states of the Middle East today. Racism there was,

in alarming quantity, but it was directed against another race and it was not merely rhetorical. The Negro suffered far more discrimination and violence than the Jew did in that era or later. Moreover, there was little in the Southern tradition to restrain the political exploitation of anti-Negro prejudice and much more to encourage its use than there was in the American tradition with respect to anti-Semitism. Racism was exploited in the South with fantastic refinements and revolting excesses in the Populist period. Modern students of the dynamics of race prejudice, such as Bruno Bettelheim and Morris Janowitz, find similarities between anti-Negro feelings and anti-Semitism and in the psychological traits of those to whom both appeal. First in the list of those traits under both anti-Negro attitudes and anti-Semitism is "the feeling of deprivation," and another lower in the list but common to both, is "economic apprehensions." The Southern Populists would seem to have constituted the perfect market for Negrophobia.

But perhaps the most remarkable aspect of the whole Populist movement was the resistance its leaders in the South put up against racism and racist propaganda and the determined effort they made against incredible odds to win back political rights for the Negroes, to defend those rights against brutal aggression, and to create among their normally anti-Negro following, even temporarily, a spirit of tolerance in which the two races of the South could work together in one party for the achievement of common ends. These efforts included not only the defense of the Negro's right to vote, but also his right to hold office, serve on juries, receive justice in the courts and defense against lynchers. The Populists failed, and some of them turned bitterly against the Negro as the cause of their failure. But in the efforts they made for racial justice and political rights they went further toward extending the Negro political fellowship, recognition and equality than any native white political movement has ever gone before or since in the South. This record is of greater historical significance and deserves more emphasis and attention than any anti-Semitic tendencies the movement manifested in that region or any other. If resistance to racism is the test of acceptability for a place in the American political heritage, Populism would seem to deserve more indulgence at the hands of its critics than it has recently enjoyed.

Two other aspects of the identification between the old Populism and the new radical right require critical modification. Talcott Parsons, Max Lerner and Victor Ferkiss, among others, find that the old regional strongholds of Populism tended to become the strongholds of isolationism in the period between the two world wars and believe there is more than a fortuitous connection between a regional proneness to Populism and isolationism. These and other critics believe also that they discern a logical connection between a regional addiction to Populism in the old days and to McCarthyism in recent times.

In both of these hypotheses the critics have neglected to take into account the experience of the South and mistakenly assumed a strong Populist heritage in the Middle West. One of the strongest centers of Populism, if not the strongest, the South in the foreign policy crisis before the Second World War was the least isolationist and the most internationalist and interventionist part of the country. And after the war, according to Nathan Glazer and Seymour Lipset, who base their statement on opinion poll studies, "the South was the most anti-McCarthy section of the country." It is perfectly possible that in rejecting isolationism and McCarthyism the South was "right" for the "wrong" reasons, traditional and historical reasons. V. O. Key has suggested that among the reasons for its position on foreign policy were centuries of dependence on world trade, the absence of any concentration of Irish or Germanic popu-

lation, and the predominantly British origin of the white population. Any adequate explanation of the South's rejection of McCarthy would be complex, but part of it might be the region's peculiarly rich historical experience with its own assortment of demagogues— Populistic and other varieties—and the consequent acquirement of some degree of sophistication and some minimal standards of decency in the arts of demagoguery. No one has attempted to explain the South's anti-isolationism and anti-McCarthyism by reference to its Populist heritage—and certainly no such explanation is advanced here.

To do justice to the new critique of Populism it should be acknowledged that much of its bill of indictment is justified. It is true that the Populists were a provincial lot and that much of their thinking was provincial. It is true that they took refuge in the agrarian myth, that they denied the commercial character of agricultural enterprise and sometimes dreamed of a Golden Age. In their economic thought they overemphasized the importance of money and oversimplified the nature of their problems by claiming a harmony of interest between farmer and labor, by dividing the world into "producers" and "nonproducers," by reducing all conflict to "just two sides," and by thinking that too many ills and too many remedies of the world were purely legislative. Undoubtedly many of them were fascinated with the notion of conspiracy and advanced conspiratorial theories of history, and some of them were given to apocalyptic premonitions of direful portent.

To place these characteristics in perspective, however, one should inquire how many of them are peculiar to the Populists and how many are shared by the classes or groups or regions or by the period to which the Populists belong. The great majority of Populists were provincial, ill-educated and rural, but so were the great majority of Americans in the nineties, Republicans and Democrats as well. They were heirs to all the superstition, folklore and prejudice that is the heritage of the ill-informed. The Populists utilized and institutionalized some of this, but so did their opponents. There were a good many conspiratorial theories and economic nostrums and oversimplifications adrift in the latter part of the nineteenth century, and the Populists had no monopoly of them. They did overemphasize the importance of money, but scarcely more so than did their opponents, the Gold Bugs. The preoccupation with monetary reforms and remedies was a characteristic of the period rather than a peculiarity of the Populists. The genuine Populist, moreover, was more concerned with the "primacy of credit" than with the "primacy of money," and his insistence that the federal government was the only agency powerful enough to provide a solution for the agricultural credit problem proved to be sound. And so did his contention that the banking system was stacked against his interest and that reform in this field was overdue.

The Populist doctrine of a harmony of interest between farmer and labor, between workers and small businessmen, and the alignment of these "producers" against the parasitic "nonproducers," is not without precedent in our political history. Any party that aspires to gain power in America must strive for a coalition of conflicting interest groups. The Populist effort was no more irrational in this respect than was the Whig coalition and many others, including the New Deal coalition.

The political crises of the nineties evoked hysterical responses and apocalyptic delusions in more than one quarter. The excesses of the leaders of a protest movement of provincial, unlettered and angry farmers are actually more excusable and understandable than the rather similar responses of the spokesmen of the educated, successful and privileged classes of the urban East. There would seem to be less excuse for hysteria and conspiratorial obsessions among the latter. One

thinks of the *Nation* describing the Sherman Silver Purchase Act as a "socialistic contrivance of gigantic proportions," or of Police Commissioner Theodore Roosevelt declaring in "the greatest soberness" that the Populists were "plotting a social revolution and the subversion of the American Republic" and proposing to make an example of twelve of their leaders by "shooting them dead" against a wall. Or there was Joseph H. Choate before the Supreme Court pronouncing the income tax "the beginnings of socialism and communism" and "the destruction of the Constitution itself." For violence of rhetoric *Harper's Weekly,* the New York *Tribune* and the Springfield *Republican* could hold their own with the wool-hat press in the campaign of 1896. Hysteria was not confined to mugwump intellectuals with status problems. Mark Hanna told an assembly of his wealthy friends at the Union League Club they were acting like "a lot of scared hens."

Anarchism was almost as much a conspiracy symbol for conservatives as Wall Street was for the Populists, and conservatives responded to any waving of the symbol even more irrationally, for there was less reality in the menace of anarchism for capitalism. John Hay had a vituperative address called "The Platform of Anarchy" that he used in the campaign of 1896. The Springfield *Republican* called Bryan "the exaltation of anarchy"; Dr. Lyman Abbott labeled Bryanites "the anarchists of the Northwest," and Dr. Charles H. Parkhurst was excited about the menace of "anarchism" in the Democratic platform. It was the Populist sympathizer Governor John Peter Altgeld of Illinois who pardoned the three anarchists of Haymarket, victims of conservative hysteria, and partly corrected the gross miscarriage of justice that had resulted in the hanging of four others. The New York *Times* promptly denounced Governor Altgeld as a secret anarchist himself, and Theodore Roosevelt said that Altgeld would conspire to inaugurate "a red government of lawlessness and dishonesty as fantastic and vicious as the Paris Commune." There was more than a touch of conspiratorial ideology in the desperate conservative reaction to the agrarian revolt. An intensive study of the nineties can hardly fail to leave the impression that this decade had rather more than its share of zaniness and crankiness, and that these qualities were manifested in the higher and middling as well as the lower orders of American society.

Venturing beyond the 1890's and speaking of populists with a small *p,* some of the new critics would suggest that popular protest movements of the populistic style throughout our history have suffered from a peculiar addiction to scares, scapegoats and conspiratorial notions. It is true that such movements tend to attract the less sophisticated, the people who are likely to succumb to cranks and the appeal of their menaces and conspiratorial obsessions. But before one accepts this as a populistic or radical peculiarity, one should recall that the Jacobin Scare of the 1790's was a Federalist crusade and that the populistic elements of that era were its victims and not its perpetrators. One should remember also that A. Mitchell Palmer and the super-patriots who staged the Great Red Scare of 1919–1920 were not populistic in their outlook. One of the most successful conspiratorial theories of history in American politics was the Great Slave Conspiracy notion advanced by the abolitionists and later incorporated in the Republican Party credo for several decades.

Richard Hofstadter has put his finger on a neglected tendency of some Populists and Progressives as well, the tendency he calls "deconversion from reform to reaction," the tendency to turn cranky, illiberal and sour. This happened with disturbing frequency among leaders as well as followers of Populism. Perhaps the classic example is the Georgia Populist Tom Watson, twice his

party's candidate for President and once for Vice-President. When Watson soured he went the whole way. By no means all of the Populist leaders turned sour, but there are several other valid instances. Even more disturbing is the same tendency to turn sour among the old Populist rank and file, to take off after race phobias, religious hatreds and witch hunts. The reasons for this retrograde tendency among reformers to embrace the forces they have spent years in fighting have not been sufficiently investigated. It may be that in some instances the reform movement appeals to personalities with unstable psychological traits. In the case of the Populists, however, it would seem that a very large part of the explanation lies in embittered frustration—repeated and tormenting frustration of both the leaders and the led.

Whatever the explanation, it cannot be denied that some of the offshoots of Populism are less than lovely to contemplate and rather painful to recall. Misshapen and sometimes hideous, they are caricatures of the Populist ideal, although their kinship with the genuine article is undeniable. No one in his right mind can glory in their memory, and it would at times be a welcome relief to renounce the whole Populist heritage in order to be rid of the repulsive aftermath. Repudiation of the Populist tradition presents the liberal-minded Southerner in particular with a temptation of no inconsiderable appeal, for it would unburden him of a number of embarrassing associations.

In his study of populist traits in American society, Edward Shils has some perceptive observations on the difficult relations between politicians and intellectuals. He adds a rather wistful footnote: "How painful the American situation looked to our intellectuals when they thought of Great Britain. There the cream of the graduates of the two ancient universities entered the civil service by examinations which were delightfully archaic and which had no trace of spoils patronage about them. . . . Politics, radical politics, conducted in a seemly fashion by the learned and reflective was wonderful. It was an ideal condition which was regretfully recognized as impossible to reproduce in the United States." He himself points out many of the reasons why this is possible in Britain, the most dignified member of the parliamentary fraternity: respect for "betters," mutual trust within the ruling classes, deferential attitudes of working class and middle class, the aura of aristocracy and monarchy that still suffuses the institutions of a government no longer aristocratic, the retention of the status and the symbols of hierarchy despite economic leveling. No wonder that from some points of view, "the British system seemed an intellectual's paradise."

America has it worse—or at least different. The deferential attitude lingers only in the South, and there mainly as a quaint gesture of habit. Respect for "betters" is un-American. Glaring publicity replaces mutual trust as the *modus vivendi* among the political elite. No aura of aristocratic decorum and hierarchal sanctity surrounds our governmental institutions, even the most august of them. Neither Supreme Court nor State Department nor Army is immune from popular assault and the rude hand of suspicion. The sense of institutional identity is weak, and so are institutional loyalties. Avenues between the seats of learning and the seats of power are often blocked by mistrust and mutual embarrassment.

America has no reason to expect that it could bring off a social revolution without a breach of decorum or the public peace, nor that the revolutionary party would eventually be led by a graduate of exclusive Winchester and Oxford. American politics are not ordinarily "conducted in a seemly fashion by the learned and reflective." Such success as we have enjoyed in this respect—the instances of the Sage of Monticello and the aristocrat of Hyde Park come to mind—have to be ac-

counted for by a large element of luck. Close investigation of popular upheavals of protest and reform in the political history of the United States has increasingly revealed of late that they have all had their seamy side and their share of the irrational, the zany and the retrograde. A few of the more successful movements have borrowed historical reputability from the memory of the worthies who led them, but others have not been so fortunate either in their leaders or their historians.

One must expect and even hope that there will be future upheavals to shock the seats of power and privilege and furnish the periodic therapy that seems necessary to the health of our democracy. But one cannot expect them to be any more decorous or seemly or rational than their predecessors. One can reasonably hope, however, that they will not all fall under the sway of the Huey Longs and Father Coughlins who will be ready to take charge. Nor need they if the tradition is maintained which enabled a Henry George to place himself in the vanguard of the antimonopoly movement in his day, which encouraged a Henry Demarest Lloyd to labor valiantly to shape the course of Populism, or which prompted an Upton Sinclair to try to make sense of a rag-tag-and-bob-tail aberration in California.

For the tradition to endure, for the way to remain open, however, the intellectual must not be alienated from the sources of revolt. It was one of the glories of the New Deal that it won the support of the intellectual and one of the tragedies of Populism that it did not. The intellectual must resist the impulse to identify all the irrational and evil forces he detests with such movements because some of them, or the aftermath or epigone of some of them, have proved so utterly repulsive. He will learn all he can from the new criticism about the irrational and illiberal side of Populism and other reform movements, but he cannot afford to repudiate the heritage.

WILLIAM P. TUCKER (b. 1910) is a professor of political
science at the University of Puerto Rico. In this essay he
analyzes the Ferkiss argument plank by plank and leaves
little doubt as to his estimate of Populism. The merits of this
brief rejoinder lie not in the advancement of any new line of
thinking, but in the pointed character of his rebuttal to the
revisionists. *

William P. Tucker

Ezra Pound, Fascism, and Populism

The influence of prominent "non-political" people on political thought and action is indeed a significant theme for political science research. It is, in fact, an area that could profitably receive much more attention than it has attracted in the past. Professor Ferkiss' study of "Ezra Pound and American Fascism" (*The Journal of Politics*, May, 1955) is an able example of such an evaluation. The author analyzes Pound's basic philosophy as related to his poetry and economic thought, his economic thought, his interpretation of history, his political philosophy, and his anti-Semitism.

Despite the cogency of the author's analysis in general, I have the feeling that his analogies between American fascism and assumed characteristics of American populism are overdrawn. Ferkiss says: "American fascism had its roots in American populism; it pursued the same ends and even used many of the same slogans. Both despaired of achieving a just society under the joined banners of liberalism and capitalism. The attacks on finance capitalism, the hatred of social democracy and socialism, the belief that representative democracy is a mask for rule by a predatory economic plutocracy, and that a strong executive is essential for the creation and preservation of a middle-class society composed of small independent landowners, suspicion of freedom of the press and civil lib-

---

* William P. Tucker, "Ezra Pound, Fascism, and Populism," *The Journal of Politics*, XVIII (February, 1956), 105–107.

erties generally as the shields and instrumentalities of the plutocracy, ultra-nationalism, anti-Semitism (both latent and active), and, finally, a peculiar interpretation of history which sees in events a working-out of a dialectic which opposes the financier and producer—these populist beliefs and attitudes form the core of Pound's philosophy, just as they provide the basis of American fascism generally."

This is a very broad indictment and takes in a lot of ground. Certain parallels can be drawn between many and diverse social movements, but I doubt that many and important roots of American fascism can be traced to American populism. (A number of important social security services were established in Germany and Russia before their adoption in the United States, but I doubt if the direct influence of the former was great on the latter.)

Ferkiss says that both American fascism and populism "despaired of achieving a just society under the joined banners of liberalism and capitalism." Twentieth century thought probably goes a long way toward agreeing with the populist criticism of the 1890's against the shortcomings of the rugged-individualist "liberalism" of that day. What might be interpreted as attacks on "finance capitalism" or some of its aspects were made by the populists—and earlier by the Farmers Alliances, state Granger parties, and other third parties—and later by various parties up through the La Follette platform of 1924. Even the major parties, for example, called for much more vigorous anti-trust law enforcement and utility regulation; the Populists of 1892 and La Follette in 1924 called for public ownership of railroads—with both demanding interestingly similar safeguards against possible governmental bureaucratic evils. Today, recognition of the essentially middle-class reformist (not radical) character of populism is reflected in historians Morison's and Commager's comment on the

1892 platform that "within a generation almost every one of the planks had been incorporated into law in whole or in part."

Even less than serious "attacks on finance capitalism" do I find Populist-produced "hatred of social democracy and socialism. . . ." Populist literature is short on comments on doctrinaire socialist ideology and parties. In terms of public ownership and other social legislation, we can find important similarities between the two ideologies; but nowhere do I find any significant amount of populist "hatred of social democracy and socialism."

It is true that the 1892 platform says that "Corruption dominates the ballot box, the Legislatures, the Congress, and touches even the ermine of the bench." But this can hardly be equated with Professor Ferkiss' "belief that representative democracy is a mask for rule by a predatory economic plutocracy," except in the sense that representative government was considered as having been perverted by "predatory wealth," with the people largely unaware.

Populist thought was not given to elaborating logical programs of doctrine on "civil liberties"—or other aspects of political philosophy, for that matter, except in so far as such concepts seemed to bear an important relation to economic doctrine. One example was populist support of labor's freedom to organize effectively.

I would not concur in the statement that populism resembled fascism in calling for a strong executive. In fact, populist literature at various times called for the direct election of the President and the Vice President—as well as of Senators and federal judges—the better to hold these officials accountable to the people. The direct primary was also espoused, as were the Australian ballot, woman suffrage, direct legislation, and the easy amendment of state constitutions. As one historian of populism stated, in order to attack monopoly, "to break its hold on the government, and to apply its collectivist program, it was necessary that the government be fully and continually responsive to the public will." Hence, the espousal of such measures as those mentioned above.

Professor Ferkiss holds that "Significantly, most of the old Populist strongholds and the political leaders bred of them were bitter-end isolationists and carried their nationalism to the point of receptivity to economic apologias for the fascist powers not unlike those used by Pound." I feel that this charge would need some documentation. It was true that the Middle West was considered more isolationist than the rest of the country until after 1940, but public opinion polls in recent years show no drastic difference from the rest of the country on foreign policy matters. As for "most of the old Populist strongholds and the political leaders bred of them . . . [being] bitter isolationists," we should not forget that populism had considerable influence in the South and the South has long been one of our least isolationist areas.

There remains the charge of "anti-Semitism (both latent and active)" against the populists. I think there is a small measure of validity here. At one stage or another of their careers, some leaders like Tom Watson and Ignatius Donnelly reflected varying degrees of anti-Semitism in their writings. But there is little evidence of any substantial reflection of such thought among the rank and file or in the general populist literature. And it seems doubtful that the virus was any more widespread than in some more polite circles. (See, for example, Henry James' comment on what he regarded as "the extent of the Hebrew conquest of New York. . . .")

These comments on populism are not meant to detract from the significance of Professor Ferkiss' article. His study is indeed worth while and it should serve as a stimulus to other similar studies.

In *The Tolerant Populists* (1963) WALTER T. K.
NUGENT (b. 1935), of Indiana University, examines the
revisionist argument in the light of the Kansas experience.
Unlike earlier writers on the subject, he has analyzed the
foreign language press. His observations on anti-Semitism
and antiforeignism stand out in sharp contrast to those of
Ferkiss and Hofstadter. He feels that the revisionists have
made some contributions. *

Walter T. K. Nugent

The Tolerant Populists

The Populists have been accused of nativism, both of a personal kind and of an ideological kind; instead, they were friendlier
and more receptive to foreign persons and
foreign institutions than the average of their
contemporary political opponents. They have
been accused of "conspiracy-mindedness";
for them, however, tangible fact quite eclipsed
neurotic fiction. They have been accused of anti-Semitism, both personal and
ideological; instead they consistently got
along well with their Jewish neighbors and
consistently refrained from extending their
dislike of certain financiers, who happened to
be Jews, to Jews in general. They have been
accused of chauvinism and jingoism, especially with reference to the Spanish-American
War; instead, such lukewarm support as they
gave collectively to Cuban intervention was
based on quite different grounds, and as a
group they strongly opposed the imperialism
that the war engendered. Finally, they have
been accused of selling out their vaunted
reform principles by seeking political fusion
with the Democratic party, especially in
1896, and thus of revealing a neurotic instability; but instead, fusion was for them a
legitimate means to the accomplishment of
real, if limited, reform. In the case of Kansas,
the largest of the wheat-belt Populist states,
the five principal criticisms of Populism
voiced by recent writers not only do not

* Reprinted from *The Tolerant Populists* by Walter T. K. Nugent by permission of The University of Chicago
Press. Copyright © 1963 by the University of Chicago. Pp. 231–236.

square with the facts, but should be replaced with a viewpoint so much in contrast as to be practically the opposite. Briefly put, this viewpoint is as follows.

Populism in Kansas was a political response to economic distress. From the early days of the Farmers' Alliance, the progenitor of the People's party, to about 1892, relief of economic difficulty was virtually the sole reason for the party's existence; after 1892 this purpose was alloyed to some degree with the desire of the party to perpetuate itself as a political organism. In both periods, however, economic difficulties remained the party's chief reason for being, and relief of them its main objective. Populism called for the enactment of a set of legislative reforms by state and federal governments and accepted the extension of governmental power involved in such enactment. In its most complete and ideal form, the Populist program appeared in the national party platform of 1892, the "Omaha Platform," but this platform bore no more nor less relation to the practical operations of the party than platforms usually do. In Kansas the People's party placed its emphasis consistently on the three questions of land, money, and transportation, which were the issues causing greatest distress in that particular state. Since monetary reform seemed to have the broadest political appeal of all the reforms called for in the Populist program, it received more stress than the rest of the program at the time (1894–97) when the party seemed to have its best chance of succeeding.

As Populism followed the ways of practical party politics in the program that it offered and in the issues it chose to stress, it took a practical approach to its sources of support as well. Economic distress cut across lines of religion, of nationality origins, of race, of previous political affiliation, even of occupation and of wealth and status. To so great an extent was this the case that it is not even accurate to say that the Populists accepted or

sought the support of third-party men, Republicans, Democrats, immigrants of many kinds, organized labor, city dwellers, and others, to broaden their agriculturalist base. For these groups were in and of Populism from the beginning. The job of the party leaders was therefore not so much to attract new groups but to be sure that the party program appealed to each of those groups already there and to spread the Populist message to further individual members of the existing coalition, of which the lowest common denominator was a desire for one or more specific economic reforms.

As a result, large numbers of every politically consequential foreign-born group then in Kansas, with the exception of the Mennonites, became active Populists. Party leaders received this support warmly and eagerly, except for one or two occasions: the 1894 state convention and probably the one of 1890. At those times, certain influential leaders supported the non-economic issues of women's suffrage and prohibition so vocally that they led the party to take positions unacceptable to many foreign-born groups. Even here, however, the attitude of these leaders to the foreign-born was one of indifference not of hostility. The fact of the matter seems to be, to judge by statements made by the delegates on the floor of the 1894 convention, that many Populists were simply unconcerned with ethnic groups or foreign matters; they were neither favorable nor hostile, except when they thought they might justifiably appeal to ethnic bloc votes or when they cited examples of enlightened foreign institutions to document their own reform program. To the great majority of Populists, in 1894 and at other times, foreignness and certainly Jewishness were simply not affective categories. For practical political reasons, among others, the Populists expressed themselves favorably toward foreign groups, either abroad or close at hand. This was certainly true of the fusionists; it was true of the non-fusionists except when women's suffrage and prohibition got in the way; it was even true, at times, of the Middle-of-the-Road group, which combined an antibanker (including English, Anglo-Jewish, and Wall Street banker) rhetoric with some benevolence toward immigrants as individuals.

Many leading Populists were in fact first or second generation immigrants. In the 1890's the Populists surpassed the Republicans in the proportion of their state legislators who were foreign-born. Foreign-born Populists abounded among county-level officeholders, county committeemen, precinct workers, and delegates to county, district, and state political conventions. Wherever an ethnic group existed, there existed as well its Populist voters and Populist leaders, with the exception of the Mennonites, who were undeviatingly Republican. The Populists, however, had immigrant blocs of their own, especially on the frequent occasions of county and state-level fusion with the Democrats. The party organization appealed to foreign-language groups with pamphlets, newspapers, and campaign speakers. They presented much the same arguments to their polyglot audience as the party was making to the English-speaking voters. The only difference was in window dressing, such as testimonials from Prince Bismarck and from German political economists in support of silver coinage. At their 1894 state convention, and prior and subsequently in their newspapers, the Populists forthrightly condemned the American Protective Association, the most influential and widespread nativist organization since the Know-Nothings.

On three contemporaneous issues relating directly to immigrants, the Populists took positions that might seem at first glance to have been nativistic, but in each case their attitude to the immigrant was neutral or favorable. When they attacked "alien" landholding, they were attacking landlordism, not the immigrant small landholder. When

they called for an end to contract or "pauper labor" immigration, they clearly excepted "worthwhile" or "sturdy" immigrants and based their position on labor competition, not on racism. When their congressmen supported the Lodge-McCall literacy test to restrict immigration, they apparently did so as the only practical way to enact the bill's riders, which would have lessened labor competition, and almost never expressed approval of the philosophy of superior and inferior, desirable or undesirable, races put forward by Lodge and the Immigration Restriction League. In each of these three instances the Populists based their actions on reasonable economic grounds, if not especially perceptive or laudable ones. Their aim was to attract the political support of organized labor, of tenant farmers, and very likely of Irish-Americans.

The rhetoric of Populism was highly charged with nationalism, but it was a nineteenth-century kind of nationalism that did not include the nativistic or anti-Semitic characteristics of some twentieth-century right-wing nationalists. Only two foreign groups fell under the censure of any considerable number of Populists. This censure was a consequence of two issues firmly rooted in economic realities and in neither case did they grow out of or were they extended to racial or nativistic antagonism. The two groups were English or Anglo-Jewish financiers and English or Anglo-Irish landlords, respectively responsible in part for money stringency and for large landholding. Many Populists feared that the trend toward tighter money and tighter land would continue unchecked unless these two groups, *and their American or Gentile associates*, were stopped. In both cases the antipathy of the Populists clearly extended to all malevolent financiers, monopolists, and land barons, whether English or American, whether Jew or Gentile, whether native or alien. For the Populists, or many of them, to have laid their troubles at the door of a mixed group of English, Anglo-Jewish, and American capitalists may have been naive and simplistic, but the point is that the common denominator of their hostility was not nativism or anti-Semitism but distrust and dislike of a truly unsympathetic economic class. In some cases their anti-English attitude transcended this economic base, since the economic problem meshed so well with the rather widespread anti-English attitude shared by many nineteenth-century Americans as part of the American Revolutionary tradition. But the English people escaped the censure placed upon certain financially powerful Englishmen, and Jewish financiers escaped any blame whatever as Jews, although a few of them, as investment bankers, shared the criticisms heaped by the Populists, or rather, some of their more outspoken rhetoricians, upon the wickedness of powerful financial interests in general. This was certainly the case with the terms "Shylock" and "Rothschild," which appeared with some frequency in Populist literature but which were cachets not of Jewish conspiracy but of oppressive finance.

So far did Populist expressions of friendliness to Jews as individuals, in Kansas and elsewhere, to Jews as a group, to English immigrants, to English institutions such as co-operatives and public ownership of utilities, outweigh the expressions that might be construed with effort as Anglophobic, anti-Semitic, and so specious are the grounds upon which the Populists have been accused of Anglophobia, anti-Semitism, or nativism, that these accusations must simply fall without support. There is an exception that proves the rule. A handful of Populists sometimes let their antipathies include "racial characteristics" of these two groups, especially the English, and thereby they evidenced irrationality and prejudice. They were atypical. Many, in fact nearly all, of these Populists were attached to the Middle-of-the-Road Populist splinter group in 1894 and

1896. This group attempted to overthrow the recognized state leadership, whose reform credentials were at least as old and respectable as the dissidents'; it was in all probability subsidized by the Republican state organization; and it received the support of less than 1 per cent of the rank and file at the polls in 1896 and of the Populist press.

In what, then, did their nationalism consist? It is difficult to answer such a question, because to accuse such a pragmatic, anti-intellectual people as these agrarians of having possessed "concepts" or "ideas," much more a "system," is itself a distortion. They did, however, possess felt attitudes that were forced into words to form the rhetoric of their speeches and editorials. Needless to say, the scribes and leaders of Populism came closer than anyone else to expressing these views in logical form, subject, of course, to political exigencies. But it can be assumed that their rhetoric must have been congenial to the rank and file—otherwise they would have been unable to attract and to hold that rank and file. Nonetheless, the rhetoric is undoubtedly more radical, more logically organized, and much more explicit than the views of the mass of the party. In their rhetoric, Populist nationalism consisted of a feeling that the United States was a different *kind* of political society from any that had ever existed before and therefore more worth preserving than any previous one. America was not just another nation-state but an embodiment of certain ideals. It was the embodiment of democratic republicanism: a society where the people rule, where the governed consent to their governors, where the rights of life, liberty, and property are protected because this very protection is the object of their own self-government. It was the embodiment, too, of economic democracy: where resources wanted only honest labor to be translated into the reality of abundance, where opportunity was equal, where the distribution of the nation's wealth was equitable. It was the antithesis of Europe and Europe's corruption, decadence, parasitical upper classes, stagnation, and economic and political oppression. It was a place, in short, where the people rule for themselves and for the protection of their natural rights. Or, at least, so it should have been.

Yet who were the people? The answer is already implied. The people were those who believed in the ideals of democratic republicanism, of economic democracy, and of freedom from European conditions of life. The people were those who actively sought the preservation of those ideals. They were those who labored by their own hands, who had equal opportunities to labor and to accumulate, who used the resources of the United States to produce their own and the nation's wealth. They were those who created wealth rather than those who manipulated wealth already produced. Very often this legitimate wealth-producing activity was defined by the Populists as agricultural and laboring activity; those who farmed or labored were by definition the real people. This corresponded conveniently both to what might roughly be called the Jeffersonian-Jacksonian tradition and to the actual political bases of the People's party's support. Translated into the rhetoric of a political campaign, it often meant emphasizing "the producing classes" or the common bonds of "the farming and laboring people."

The conscious derivation for all of this was the American Revolution, and secondarily, the War of 1812. These struggles successfully created a nation embodying this set of ideals. Such conscious roots made it easy, of course, for some Populists to look upon the machinations of English financiers as a third and final attempt by England to subjugate America. It was primarily through the American Revolution that a nation of, by, and for the people was created and through it that all that was wrong with Europe and Britain was left behind.

Consequently, it was up to the people—often implying the farmers and laborers—to see to it that this nation, this unique society, did not perish from the earth. Who threatened its extinction? Certainly not the refugee from European misery, at least so long as he, too, believed in American republicanism and opportunity. In this unique kind of nation the doors were open to those who wished legitimately to share its benefits. The goods of this nation were not to be shut up inside for the exclusive use of those already there but rather to beckon as to a flourishing haven those who wished to escape the oppression of a decadent Europe. The nation was, in Lincoln's words, a last, best hope of earth. The immigrant was to show his good faith in these ideals by becoming a citizen and remaining permanently (as the Populists' alien land law provided) and by not attempting to destroy the opportunity of individuals already possessing it (as Populist demands for an end to "pauper labor" immigration showed). For an immigrant to take away the job of an American laborer was unnecessary anyway, since opportunity and America were virtually synonymous.

The "worthwhile" or "sturdy" immigrant was not, then, the enemy of American nationality. In fact, he seemed to justify the Populist approach to American nationality—certainly he did in the case of immigrant agricultural colonies in Kansas, which had been very successful—and he was therefore quite welcome. But who then *was* the enemy? To most Populists who thought about the matter beyond their immediate economic distress—and by no means all of them thought through their views of American nationalism with anything like the completeness that this sketch might imply—the enemy lay in certain recently emergent opportunities for malevolence. America was shifting from a predominantly rural and agricultural nation to one predominantly urban and industrial. This shift was in no way evil in itself. Populist spokesmen such as Senators Peffer and Harris had expressly denied any hope of turning back the clock, and if they were not absolutely delighted with a process that seemed to be toppling the farmers and their allies from political and economic predominance (if indeed they had ever possessed it), they were determined to live with such a trend. What is more, they were determined to see that these changes should benefit all the people and not just a few; that they should take place in such ways as to guarantee democratic republicanism and economic democracy. The majority of them therefore accepted industrialization but condemned monopoly, accepted banking and finance but condemned usury and financial sleight of hand, welcomed accumulation but condemned economic feudalism, welcomed enterprise but condemned speculation. It was not industry and urbanism that oppressed them, they thought, but their abuse.

For most Populists these considerations identified the enemy well enough. An appealing program, aimed conveniently at the relief of immediate distress as well as at the placing of new trends within the old ideals, could be constructed without further ado. A rhetoric quickly emerged that concerned itself with attacking landlordism, transportation monopoly, and money shortages, and this rhetoric remained the basic vehicle of Populist ideas from start to finish. In a minority of cases, however, it seemed convenient to personalize the enemy, and in doing so, some Populists passed the bounds of precise statement. At times, American financiers and monopolists such as the Belmonts, Morgans, and Vanderbilts, English financiers such as the Rothschilds, American and English land and mortgage loan companies, and prominent American statesmen such as Sherman, McKinley, and Cleveland, together seemed to form a common and inimical class dedicated to the people's overthrow. Ever since the Civil War this group seemed to have conspired to bring about the economic destruction of the farmers and their allies. This minority of Populists thereby dealt with the money question in terms of a "money power." Yet even they nearly all used the term "conspiracy" in a general sense to mean the common attitudes of an entrenched and powerful minority, and only a tiny proportion meant by the term an explicit conspiratorial agreement, as when they referred to Ernest Seyd and the "Hazzard Circular" of the sixties and seventies. But most Populists did not voice this line, a fact more remarkable if one grants that rhetoric tends to be more radical than the general feeling of its political following. This "conspiracy" was, in addition, a financial one and not a Jewish or English one. To look at a close-knit community of interest and to see in the mind's eye a conspiracy is not necessarily great irrationality but rather a lack of factual knowledge about the competitive methods of late nineteenth-century capitalism. If antibanker, antimonopoly, or anticapitalist statements formed fairly frequent themes in Populist rhetoric, Populists of every hue made it clear that it was usury, irresponsible economic power, and minority rule that they were opposing and not the industrial revolution, urbanism, or capitalism and banking as such. The abuse of new trends, not the trends themselves had driven them, they felt, from their once uncontested eminence. Now they wanted to regain that eminence and accepted the fact that it could never again be theirs alone. If agrarian class predominance was over and done with, plutocratic class predominance should be scuttled before it progressed any further. Then economic democracy would be reborn.

The Populist view of American nationality, with its stress on democratic republicanism and economic democracy, was therefore intended to be at once majoritarian, individualistic, and humanitarian. That it was a nationalism naïvely humanitarian rather than aggressive appeared very clearly in the

Populists' approach to the Cuban insurrection and the Spanish-American War. They sympathized deeply with the insurgent Cubans and viewed their uprising as a struggle for freedom and democracy much like the American uprising of the 1770's. In Kansas this sympathy expressed itself in a moral support for the insurrectionists that sprang from a confident view of their own moral righteousness. Nonetheless, the Populist press and Populist congressmen held back from armed intervention, took a cautious attitude to the blowing up of the *Maine,* restrained themselves from anything more vigorous than sympathetic gestures toward the Cubans in spite of the Spanish "despotism" and "Weylerism" they believed the Cubans to be suffering, and in unison with their Democratic neighbors hoped that war could be avoided. This was very close to the Republican position also. When war came, they supported it as everyone else did, but until then their humanitarian sympathy for the Cubans was checked by the fear that a war beginning with Cuban intervention could only benefit large financial interests. The Kansas Republicans' coolness toward Cuban intervention resulted mainly from the caution that McKinley maintained into April, 1898, and the desire of the Kansas Republicans to support their own administration. The Populists avoided the Republicans' scornful references to Cuban or Spanish racial inferiority and far more frequently than the Republicans took a humanitarian view of the matter. In Kansas the Populists were not violent jingoes. Furthermore, unlike the Republicans in their area, and other people elsewhere, the official Populist position on the question of American imperial expansion for commercial or military purposes, which arose after Dewey's victory in Manila Bay, was to join the Democrats in opposing expansion and in demanding that the United States leave the Philippines and other potential colonies alone. They were interested in the spread of American democratic ideals, in the overthrow of Spanish oppression of Cuba, if this could be done without the commitment of American armed forces, but not at all in American conquest or colonization. Populism in Kansas apparently lost many adherents because of this stand, but it remained the official party position nevertheless.

It is worth noting that Populist opposition to imperialism was much more firmly expressed than Populist sympathy to the Cuban insurrectionists, because the Democratic party was also much less firm on the latter question than on the former. As a matter of fact, official Populist rhetoric was tailored to fit the political exigencies involved in getting along with the Democrats not only on the war and imperialism issues but on most other questions as well. Political fusion with the Democrats on all levels marked Kansas Populism very strongly, and to some writers, fusion has meant that the Populists lacked any real dedication to the principles they so vigorously espoused. But the Populist movement chose political means to accomplish its program of economic reform; it was a political party, not a pressure group or an ideological front; for better or worse it therefore bound itself to use partisan methods. If one looks no further than the Omaha platform of 1892 to find out what Populism stood for and then observes that many planks in that platform were soft-pedaled in 1892 and later for the sake of fusion and political success, one might assume that Populist devotion to reform principles was a sham. But this is a superficial view. Fusion was the only apparent way to achieve any reforms, any accomplishment of any principles at all, and the degree to which the People's party was willing to fuse with the Democrats in Kansas was the degree to which it possessed political common sense. The identification of fusion with dedication to principle, rather than with a sellout, comes into even greater relief as soon as one recalls the shabby story of the

Middle-of-the-Road Populists, those self-styled simon-pure reformers who almost certainly connived at the defeat of the reform party with the local Republican organization. The prevalence of fusion sentiment indicates as well the willingness of the Populists to seek out and accept the support of the foreign-born blocs that ordinarily made their political home in the Democratic party. It also indicates their pragmatic approach to political action, their willingness to use an obvious means at hand to achieve legitimate political ends, and their flexibility, which stood in such contrast to the rigidity of the Middle-of-the-Road Populists.

The political horse sense that provided them with their receptivity to fusion was a natural outgrowth of the immediacy of the distress from which their movement sprang. It accounted, too, for the apparent anomaly of a radical program based on conservative ideals. For the Populists of Kansas were not a collection of rag-tag calamity howlers, ne'er-do-wells, and third-party malcontents, as William Allen White and others have suggested, but a large body of people of diverse occupational, wealth-holding, and status levels. As a group they were hardly distinguishable from their Republican neighbors, except for a probably higher mortgage indebtedness, and their greater degree of political and economic awareness. The great majority could be called "middle class," and they were interested in preserving what they considered to be their middle-class American ideals and substance. These were being threatened, they felt, not by the facts of industrialism and urbanism but by their existing *shape*. To change that shape, they settled upon the device of a political party.

Their view of the future was one in which many wrongs would have to be righted, many present trends would have to be redirected to conform to old ideals, for that future to become acceptable. Yet they were confident that this would happen. In several ways they were confused, ill-informed, and behind the times. They were unaware of urban problems, for example, and they never understood that money reform was basically a solution only to agricultural problems, if indeed to them, and not a solution for growing monopoly or for inequities of wealth distribution. Yet if this is true, it is true as well to acquit them of nativism, anti-Semitism, conspiracy-mindedness, jingoism, lack of principle, and of living in some neurotic agrarian dream world. They were bound together not by common neuroses but by common indebtedness, common price squeezes, common democratic and humanitarian ideals, and common wrath at the infringement of them. From this wrath rose the Farmers' Alliance, and from the Alliance their ultimate instrument of protest, the People's party. The Populists were far too concerned with land, money, and transportation, and also, later on, with the mechanics of winning and keeping public office, to have much time to worry about whether their ideals were mythical or their anxieties neurotic. Tight money and foreclosure sales were the products of nobody's imagination. Even in their rhetoric they were too busy preaching positive reforms in a depression to be concerned with racism or anti-Semitism or agrarian Arcadias; and in their practical political activities, they took all the help they could get.

The Populists were liberal nationalists bringing to radical social changes a radical response. By such means they meant to reassert what they considered to be the fundamental ideals upon which their society had previously depended—in their view of history—and must continue to depend—in their view of political philosophy. They undertook this task in the Kansas of the 1890's, with its particular kind of social structure, its particular distribution of wealth and income, its specific economic conditions, and its peculiar laws and traditions. These particularities form the limits of historical analogy, and they give no grounds for making the Populists the gawky ancestors of Father Coughlin or of Senator Joseph R. McCarthy. They make it very difficult to call the Populists the descendants of the Jeffersonians and Jacksonians or the precursors of Progressivism or the New Deal, although with these movements the Populists shared a considerable body of ideals. They make it unrealistic even to equate the Kansas Populists with Populists of other regions or other states.

This particular set of facts, however, allows the Populists of Kansas to be judged on their own grounds. The verdict is very simple. They were people who were seeking the solution of concrete economic distress through the instrumentality of a political party. By this means they would not only help themselves but they would redirect, not reverse, the unsatisfactory trends of their time to correspond with the ideals of the past. This involved profoundly the political co-operation of the foreign-born, and it involved a deep respect and receptivity for non-American institutions and ideas.

JOHN D. HICKS (b. 1890) has not participated in any of the debates growing out of the criticism of his interpretation of Populism. In "Our Pioneer Heritage: A Reconsideration," written in 1956, he states that writers before his time took "cracks" at the "agrarian myth" and other topics related to "agrarian liberalism." Some of the attacks were not new. In this article he explains, as he had not done in his previous writings, what influenced him to treat "our pioneer heritage," which goes to the essence of his interpretation of Populism, in the fashion that he did, and in what respects his views have been modified since the appearance of *The Populist Revolt* in 1931.*

John D. Hicks

The Role of Our Pioneer Heritage Re-evaluated

For the first time since it appeared I have just reread "Our Pioneer Heritage," an article I wrote for *Prairie Schooner* some thirty years ago. It wasn't a bad article. Nevertheless, I shouldn't care to have it republished in its original form, for if I were writing on the same subject today I wouldn't say the same things, and its republication might make some people think that I would. When I wrote the article I was, like most students of American history, under the spell of Frederick Jackson Turner's frontier hypothesis. I tried, or so it now seems to me, to make our pioneer background explain far more than it could explain, and probably far more than Turner meant it to explain. This was only

natural. In the 1920's the last American frontier wasn't much more than a generation gone; indeed, as a young country school-teacher in Johnson County, Wyoming, I had myself seen authentic remnants of it. Furthermore, the State of Nebraska, in which I then lived, had been through the frontier process fairly recently; some of my students had also seen it in the raw, among them Mari Sandoz, whose *Old Jules* is a classic of frontier history. It was easy then, and there, to magnify experiences that were so fresh in our memories, and that had meant so much in our lives. But, looking backward, it is now quite apparent that neither Mari Sandoz nor I would have seen things quite the same had

* From John D. Hicks, "Our Pioneer Heritage: A Reconsideration," in *Prairie Schooner*, XXX (Winter, 1956), 359–361. Copyright, 1956, by the University of Nebraska Press.

we sprung from the sidewalks of New York rather than from the soil of the prairies and the Great Plains.

This is not to say that I have turned my back on Turner, for I have not. He saw more clearly than any of his forerunners that the settlement of the continent by wave after wave of pioneers constituted the first full chapter of American history. There is still no getting away from the fact that the biggest thing going on in America during these formative years was the westward movement. It was basic and fundamental; nearly every aspect of our national life was geared to it. Nor can we easily deny that the frontier experience furnished thoughtful historians of America the pattern they needed to give unity to their theme. Through the frontier process every part of the nation was related to every other part; each separate locality, like a twig or a branch of some mighty tree, was a structural member of the one great whole. There was ample opportunity, too, in Turnerian doctrine for an explanation of regional differences; the nation might be one, but it was also a nation of sections, each of which grew from the differing combinations of circumstances, geographic and otherwise, that attended its origin. But, while these observations seem unassailable, Turner also chose to find in the frontier experience the basis for numerous traits and institutions that possibly have a far more complicated origin. The frontier no doubt had much to do with making us the kind of people we are, and with making our individualistic American democracy what it is, but other ingredients also entered into the process, such, for example, as the contributions of the immigrants, the effects of the industrial revolution, the conditions of urban life, and the closer relationships that grew up between the United States and the rest of the world. If I were writing today I would by no means ignore the frontier influence, but I would not see in it quite the complete explanation of subsequent developments that I seemed to see in it then. Time in itself tends to

work against the persistence of the pioneer heritage, for as the frontier experience recedes further and further into the background, new influences, quite unrelated to it, are bound to assert themselves, and to play an ever greater part in the making of the age in which we live.

I find also, as I reread my little essay, that I was then definitely a partisan of the agricultural interest in American life, and an unfriendly critic of business and industry. This was natural enough, considering my small-town and rural origins, and I am by no means free from the same sentiments today. But there is an additional explanation, as of the time and the place in which I wrote. Whatever good luck the farmer may have had during the first two decades of the twentieth century, he was in a bad way during the third. Worse still from his point of view, industry was enjoying a magnificent prosperity, with businessmen firmly in the saddle, riding high, wide, and handsome, as events were soon to prove, toward the panic of 1929. The farmer was an underdog, and he rather needed a friend. Moreover, the State of Nebraska, as primarily an agricultural community, had not yet begun to doubt the validity of such traditional ideas as that the farmer's way of life was the ideal way of life, and that the nation could not long be prosperous if agriculture remained in the doldrums. This over-concentration on the importance of agriculture was a kind of historical hangover. Only in the twentieth century have our urbanites become more numerous than their country cousins, and of course most of our frontiers started off as strictly farmers' frontiers. Now Hamlin Garland and many another observer had already taken a crack at what Richard Hofstadter was later to call "the agrarian myth," but to a Nebraskan of the 1920's the myth and the reality were pretty closely intertwined. It was hard to realize that industry was already far surpassing agriculture in its contributions to the American way of life, and that the future of the nation lay with the city rather than with the country. Indeed, as Hofstadter points out, the farmer was eventually to become prosperous only by accepting the techniques of business, including, if necessary, the highjacking of the federal government into granting him the same kind of subsidies that manufacturers had long obtained through protective tariffs and other special favors.

There are a good many other things about the article that I might criticize, but possibly the most important would be a sin of omission rather than of commission. Following in Turner's footsteps, I was too content to accept a strictly American interpretation of American history, and to relegate to unmerited insignificance the part played by the rest of the world in our national development. The distress of American agriculture, for example, not only in the 1920's but also as far back as the Populist and the Granger periods, probably stemmed less from the passing of free land and the wicked machinations of the industrialists than from the competition of non-American producers whose output was glutting the world's markets. Political isolationism had its counterpart in historical isolationism, a state of mind from which most American historians did not fully emerge until after the Second World War. This is not to say that Turner was not right for his time when he turned his back on a mainly European interpretation of American history in order to emphasize the greater significance of the westward look. But Turner's ideas were formulated at the end of the nineteenth century, and he spoke only for the age in which he lived. The events of the twentieth century have made us conscious of the United States as an intimate part of the whole world, and not simply as a separate national entity. What goes on elsewhere in the world has developed for us a significance that Turner could hardly have foreseen, much less one of his junior admirers.

We really have no occasion to speak disdainfully of the ideas we and others happen to have cherished several decades ago, even if we have come to think a little differently today. We did the best we could with the knowledge then at our command. We were trying to explain the age in which we lived, not some later age of which we knew nothing. "Let not the harmless, necessary word 'myth' put us out of countenance," Carl Becker once observed. "In the history of history a myth is a once discarded version of the human story, as our now valid version will in due course be relegated to the category of once discarded myths." The frontier myth, the agrarian myth, the isolationist myth were all in their day the most rugged realities. Who knows but in some future age bright and beaming young historians will be ringing the changes on the urban myth, the industrial myth, and the international myth?

Still another to be drawn into the controversy is
THEODORE SALOUTOS (b. 1910), a professor of history
at the University of California, Los Angeles, and a graduate
student of John Hicks at the University of Wisconsin. He is
coauthor of *Agricultural Discontent in the Middle West,
1900–1939* (1951) and author of *Farmer Movements in the
South, 1865–1933* (1964) and other works on farm unrest. The
following essay is based on an examination of the scholarly
writings on Populism, with emphasis on those published after
the standard interpretation came under attack. It reviews the
origins of the controversy and argues that the Populists were
under attack from the beginning. *

Theodore Saloutos

The Professors and the Populists

The populists were a conspicuous part of
the general reform movement that swept the
country during the closing decades of the
nineteenth century. . . . The main difference
between the Populists and other reformers of
the day is that the Populists retained their
faith in the political process and believed that
a new party, divorced from the corruptive influence of the old, would be more responsive
to the needs of the people and would deliver
them from their oppressors. . . . Being reformers, they naturally stirred up a storm of
controversy.

Among those who joined the first debates
in the 1890's and argued whether the Populists were a constructive force were the

members of the academic profession. They
joined the debates for various reasons. Some
were deeply concerned over matters of public
policy and had hopes of influencing the voters
and lawmakers by their arguments. Some
confined themselves to making scholarly in-
quiries into the developmental aspects of
thought and action in agriculture. Some felt
that as citizens they had a social obligation to
perform in discussing the issues. But,
whatever their reasons or views, they displayed deep concern over the current and
future status of the farmers who then comprised the bulk of the population and how the
populist program, if placed into operation,
would affect agriculture and the general

---

* From Theodore Saloutos, "The Professors and the Populists," *Agricultural History*, XL (October, 1966),
235–254. Footnotes omitted.

economy. In short, these debates revolved around what the Populists could or could not do for the farmers and the nation.

Within recent years, the question of whether the Populists were or were not a constructive force has again come into the forefront; this time it has come to the forefront for different reasons and has been confined to the arena of academic debate. Conditions have changed considerably since the 1890's when agriculture held a pre-eminent position in the economy and the Populists were at their peak. The recent debates were not precipitated by an agricultural crisis comparable to the 1890's which would suggest a restudy of Populist formulas with the hope of finding a basis for new farm legislation. No proposal was under consideration during the 1950's for the launching of a new political party committed to a reformist program. Nor had fresh facts been unearthed in quantities that pointed to serious flaws in the standard interpretation of Populism.

What happened instead was this. Issues of peculiar concern to the academicians, not the policy makers, of the 1950's were projected back into the 1890's and buttressed with the argument that new scholarly techniques merited fresh and up-to-date conclusions that presumably escaped earlier writers. The revisionist emphasis was more on new techniques and less on fresh evidence, more on issues that were of greater concern to the scholars of the 1950's and only of peripheral interest to the Populists of the 1890's. As a consequence, the debates took a course in which the Populists, if resurrected in the 1960's, probably would have difficulty in recognizing themselves.

Most will agree that the debate over the Populists was triggered by the attempt to get at the roots of "McCarthyism" which was gnawing at the vitals of American society during the 1950's. McCarthy was no agrarian with deep attachments to the underdog finding it difficult to compete with big business and its allies. He was, first and foremost, an opportunist who cultivated the friendship of numerous wealthy individuals whose political and economic thinking was diametrically opposed to that of the Populists. Still some scholars persisted in arguing that the roots of McCarthyism were to be found in Populism. The reasoning behind this argument seemed to follow this pattern of thought: the emergence of Senator Joe McCarthy, whose home state of Wisconsin once was a hotbed of Granger agitation and isolationist sentiment and the birthplace of Senator Robert M. La Follette, Sr., suggested that this section of the country was the repository of something more hideous than the historians had told us.

But these critics have had much more to say about the Populists than merely to attempt to link them to McCarthyism. They have charged, among other things, that the earlier scholars were less critical of the Populists than the newer ones; the Populist contribution has been grossly exaggerated and should be restated with greater emphasis on the negative aspects; the Populist Party was a national party and not a sectional one; the Populists were unoriginal; the Populists were anti-foreign, anti-Semitic, and bigoted and thus qualify as forerunners of American fascism; the Populist farmers were more reformist in their orientation than the wage earners and their leaders; and the Populists were simpletons who believed in simple solutions to complex problems.

First, let us consider the supposed link between McCarthyism on the one hand and La Follette and Populism on the other. Apart from the coincidence that both La Follette and McCarthy were born in and represented the state of Wisconsin in the United States Senate and both displayed qualities of strong leadership, they were inspired by different motives, different issues, and different philosophies. La Follette, by his own admission, was greatly influenced by the Grangers, not the Populists; to him the regulation of the railroads and the curbing of their power over the government was the crying need of the day, but, unlike the Populists, he achieved his reforms by working from within the framework of one of the major parties rather than within a third party. La Follette's name never was linked with any of the leading political reactionaries of his day. McCarthy, on the other hand, was neither interested in the regulation of the railroads nor in increasing the powers of the government; his prime concern was in questioning the loyalty of top government officials and in ridding the federal government and its agencies of the Communists. The two men were poles apart in their personal behavior as well as their political thinking. If McCarthy had had his way, he probably would have undone the very authority that La Follette and his son had striven to increase.

The critics, in my opinion, have not only failed to establish a link between McCarthyism, La Follette, and Populism, but unwittingly have implied that the Populists acquired a following in Wisconsin that is totally out of proportion to reality. The peak of agrarian unrest in Wisconsin was reached during the Granger era of the 1870's and not during the Populist era of the 1890's. The record shows that the Populists polled less than three percent of the Wisconsin vote in the Presidential election of 1892, perhaps because the wheat counties which were the center of so much of the earlier farmer agitation had dwindled in number and influence. As a party, the Populists never attracted the following that the Grangers mustered in Wisconsin a generation earlier.

If the critics of the Populists insist on finding a Wisconsin link to McCarthyism, may I suggest that they look into the activities of one John B. Chapple, an obscure Ashland, Wisconsin, newspaperman with political ambitions, who travelled up and down the state during the 1930's attacking the La Fol-

lette brothers for taking the road to Communism and the University of Wisconsin for exposing the students to Communism, atheism, and free love. Chapple made many headlines in the newspapers but little political headway in a state which, for the time being, preferred to follow in the footsteps of the La Follettes; Chapple was forced to return to the same obscurity from which he emerged.

Second, were the earlier scholars of Populism less critical than the scholars of a later day? I doubt this. If anything, the evidence bears out that the professors subjected the Populists to a barrage of criticism well before the 1950's and even before 1900. With few exceptions, the first scholars were hostile. For instance, John R. Commons, an economist and economic historian of repute, long identified with progressive causes, flirted with the Populists for a time and then abandoned them on the grounds that the subtreasury plan which they were presumed to have advocated was unsound. The fact that the Populists were hopelessly divided on this issue seems to have escaped him, but this did not detract from his repudiation of them. A distinguished array of scholars, including President Francis A. Walker of Massachusetts Institute of Technology, F. W. Taussig of Harvard University, Henry C. Adams of the University of Michigan, E. R. A. Seligman of Columbia University, Richard Mayo-Smith also of Columbia University, and J. Laurence Laughlin of the University of Chicago, poured oil on the smoldering currency controversy by endorsing the repeal of the Sherman Silver Purchase Act. These men were outstanding academic figures in political economy, government, and sociology with deep roots in the historical tradition. The lines of demarcation between the different disciplines then were not as sharply drawn as they are today, and several of these scholars would have qualified as good historians.

The most outspoken contemporary critic of the Populists was J. Laurence Laughlin who got his Ph.D. in history at Harvard, switched to political economy, and taught successively at Harvard, Cornell, and the University of Chicago (where he became head of the department). Laughlin thought free silver a nostrum, a delusion, and a fantasy. He warned against "the money doctors." He met "Coin Harvey" in a debate that attracted national attention, wrote and signed editorials on the silver question for the Chicago *Times-Herald,* and encouraged his graduate students to prepare studies on the quantity theory of money that would furnish scientific arguments to be used against the silver groups. Among the budding scholars who authored such articles and published them in the *Journal of Political Economy* were Wesley C. Mitchell, who later gained fame as an authority on business cycles, and H. Parker Willis, who wrote on money and banking.

Other academicians wrote in an equally critical vein. C. F. Emerick who taught at Vanderbilt University and Smith College was unable to understand how the Populist proposal to increase the amount of money in circulation until it reached fifty dollars per capita could stimulate industrial activity. In his opinion, the Populists were beginning at the wrong end. Instead, they should have sought to aid industry obtain additional capital in the form of raw materials; once this was done, the money crisis would be alleviated. Emerick further added that these defects could be eliminated by providing for a better distribution of the banking facilities of the nation. Arthur Twining Hadley, the president of Yale University and an economist of note, although not mentioning the Populists by name, likewise dealt severely with their notions of money in a widely used college text.

Still another unsympathetic scholar was Frank LeRond McVey, whose study of *The Populist Movement* was published in the spring of 1896 by the American Economics Association. McVey cited nine planks in the Populist platform that corresponded closely with those of the Socialists and disapproved of their paternalistic philosophy. Despite his dislike of the Populists, he still believed that their principles were rooted in the American past. The McVey interpretation echoed the sentiments of many of the less articulate foes of the Populists and many conservatives who wrote for popular consumption.

Among the few academicians who openly expressed sympathy for the Populists was Frederick Emory Haynes. Haynes, instead of denouncing them as ignorant, dishonest, and malicious, studied the causes of the rise of the movement in the West and South and the nature of their grievances against the East, and he concluded that the Populists were members of the great under-represented class that was demanding greater representation in government. Unlike most scholars of his day, Haynes credited the Populists with possessing more foresight than either the Republican or Democratic parties which refused to face the pressing social and economic issues of the day.

Haynes agreed with McVey that Populism was a product of conditions prevailing in those sections of the country that grew up after the Civil War and that its program embodied many of the ingredients of Socialism. Of the latter he cited the Populist demand for government ownership of the railroads; the hostility toward banks and the agitation for an expended currency; the "reclamation of lands" owned by corporations, speculators, and aliens which he viewed as partial land nationalization; and the proposal for an income tax.

Another professor who wrote sympathetically about the Populists—at a little later time—was James Albert Woodburn who devoted the greater portion of a lengthy chapter to them in his study, *Political Parties and Problems in the United States.* To Woodburn the Populists were aggressive and outspoken on the money question and avoided the evasive "two-faced resolutions" that the two old parties employed. They knew what they believed. "The money question, in its many aspects, they looked upon as one of the greatest in the history of civilization, and as the one most vitally affecting social happiness. . . ."

The soundness of Woodburn's observations is attested to by the aggressive retaliatory tactics employed by the opponents of the Populists' monetary views. During 1895 and 1896 the Sound Currency Committee, an active anti-free silver group, printed and distributed more than 2,350,000 copies of various issues of *Sound Currency* and more than 2,000,000 copies of speeches and pamphlets. In addition, by furnishing "ready prints" and "plate matter" to newspapers that were desirous of using them, they obtained a circulation of over 48,000,000 newspaper pages, each the equivalent of a sixteen-page pamphlet. These concentrated labors on the part of the opposition are conclusive evidence that the money question was a matter of supreme importance.

Frederick Jackson Turner, unlike Haynes who viewed Populism as an attempt to resolve some of the problems that industrialism had thrust upon the nation, believed that Populism was a complex of frontier conditions—"over-confidence, reckless internal improvements, and lands purchased by borrowed capital." As was the case with McVey and Haynes, Turner also saw a relationship between Populism and Socialism. It was no surprise to him that citizens looked to the federal government

in a section whose lands were originally purchased by the government and given away to its settlers by the same authority, whose railroads were built largely by federal land grants, and whose settlements were protected by the United States Army and governed by the national authority until they

were carved into rectangular states and admitted into the Union. . . .

This, to him, was evidence of Socialism. Turner also emphasized the prevalence of lax business methods that encouraged the floating of paper money and wildcat banking. "A primitive society," added Turner, "can hardly be expected to snow an intelligent appreciation of the complexity of the business interest in a developed society."

This latter argument of Turner suggests that his money views were consistent with the conservative thinking of the day. Although he furnished a substantial, if not complete, explanation of the causes of Populism, he leaves one with the impression that he was unsympathetic with the money formulas of the Populists.

Surprisingly, Woodrow Wilson, during whose administrations as President of the United States Populism attained a higher degree of respectability, wrote, while still at Princeton, that the Populists "smacked of the extremist purpose of experiment in the field of social legislation. . . ." Theirs, added Wilson, was "a radical programme which jumped with the humor of hundreds of thousands of workingmen and farmers the country over."

Once the New Freedom was launched in 1913, the understanding and sympathy expressed earlier by Haynes and Woodburn was displayed by other scholars. Charles Beard included the Populists in his treatment of the spirit of dissent that prevailed after the Civil War in his widely used text, *Contemporary America.* In 1915 Frederic Logan Paxson devoted a full chapter of his *New Nation* to "Populism" (for all practical purposes, a narrative of the second administration of Grover Cleveland instead of a perceptive analysis of Populism), and another chapter to "Free Silver." But Paxson saw a constructive side and cogently observed that:

The mission of Populism did not end when free silver had been driven like a wedge into all the parties. Its more fundamental reforms outlasted both the hard times and the recovery from them. . . . Although obscured by the shadow of the greater controversy, the reforms had been started with conviction. The Populist party was not permitted to bring the reformation that it promised, but it stimulated within the parties in power a "counter-reformation," that was already under way. . . .

In substance, most of the earliest scholars who expressed themselves on the Populists were hostile, indifferent, or contemptuously amused by them. Haynes and Woodburn were among the first few who were sympathetic. Greater respectability for the Populists came after 1912. Unlike the critics of the 1950's and 1960's whose concern revolved around the origins of McCarthyism and whether the Populists were anti-Semitic and anti-foreign, the earlier critics concentrated on issues then considered in the mainstream of Populist thought: money, land ownership, railroad regulation, and a greater increase in the federal authority.

What about anti-Semitism and anti-foreignism? How prevalent was it among the Populists and did they use it in their propaganda? In the first place, it would be foolhardy to deny the existence of anti-foreign, anti-Semitic, and anti-Negro thought in any group—Populist and non-Populist, yet the truth of the matter is that no conclusive evidence has been uncovered to substantiate the widespread prevalence of these forms of bigotry among the Populists. Their writings and speeches convey few, if any, such sentiments. On the other hand, historians and sociologists in particular who condemn the Populists for their anti-foreign sentiments would do well to study the writings of highly respected scholars, such as John R. Commons, Edward A. Ross, Henry Pratt Fairchild, Richard Mayo-Smith, and others, the volumes of the *American Journal of Sociology,* and the annual proceedings and other publications of the American Fed-

eration of Labor. It would be much easier to find evidence of racial bigotry and anti-foreignism among scholars who taught in some of the most venerated colleges and universities of the East and other parts of the country than it would be to find comparable evidence in the writings and speeches of the Populists. If the learned men who taught the college students of their generation could be counted upon to furnish the scholarly arguments that fanned the flames of minority hatreds, what is one to expect from the thousands of poorly educated or uneducated men who swelled the ranks of Populism? If anything, the Populists should be commended, not censured, for their tolerance.

The Populist fear of the foreigner was not so much a fear of the foreigner himself as much as it was the fear of foreign corporations acquiring control of large quantities of land. If the new foreigner was to be feared he was to be feared in the large cities where he congregated in large numbers and not in agriculture which he, for the most part, avoided. Farming, after all, was a capitalistic enterprise that required large capital outlays which the average immigrant did not possess. Furthermore, farming practices in the United States differed greatly from those he knew in the old country, and the immigrant lacked the technical know-how that the average American farmer was presumed to have. Most newcomers from southern and Eastern Europe avoided the wide open spaces of the West and Southwest; they wanted to be near their compatriots who spoke the same language, observed the same customs, and worshipped in the same churches; to many of them farming was associated with hardship and despair. They also had to earn money and earn it in a hurry; agriculture did not offer them the opportunities to earn this money as quickly as the city did.

Of the earlier writers, McVey perhaps better understood the reasons for the Populist position on immigration than did some of the latter-day critics. The attacks directed against the immigration and contract laws of the United States probably were a concession to the labor leaders in attendance at the Populist conventions instead of the wish of the Populist farmers themselves. Observed McVey:

Naturally the farmer is not opposed to immigration; for he is an employer of labor, and the influx of immigrants into the more settled regions of the South and West enables him more easily to harvest the crops and enlarge his business. It is much the same as an increase of his capital, because it increases the number of laborers and thus lowers the price of labor. . . .

McVey of course, was speaking of those landowners and managers who employed labor to harvest their crops instead of the sharecroppers or small farmers who depended on their own labor and that of their families.

The contributions of the Populists to the Progressive movement also has been subjected to questioning. Much of this misunderstanding, in my opinion, stems in part from statements taken out of their context or reading into them meanings that were never intended. In 1956, twenty-five years after the appearance of *The Populist Revolt,* Hicks wrote about the Populists:

But many of their ideas lived on and greatly altered the course of 20th Century American history. The Populists helped prepare the way for Theodore Roosevelt's conservation policy, for the closer regulation of railroads and trusts, for the Federal Reserve Banking system, for a series of reforms that greatly promoted popular control of the government, both state and national, even parity prices. As a political revolt Populism was a failure; the Populist Party lived only to die. But Populism was good on diagnosis even when it was faulty on prescription. As an educational movement it was a great success.

Again, as late as 1965, Hicks observed:

Some. . .have taken my observations that many Populist demands won later acceptance to mean that I regarded nineteenth century Populism as the primary cause of twentieth century Progressivism. I would not so interpret my comments; certainly the Progressive urbanites had many quite separate reasons of their own for embracing so much of the Populist program. . . .

An examination of *The Populist Revolt* contains few, if any, suggestions that former Populists assumed commanding positions in thought and action in the Progressive movement. Many of the Populist leaders in the Middle West and South were broken in spirit and demoralized after the campaign of 1896 and gave up in despair. Some dropped out of politics completely, others returned to one of the regular parties, and still others became Socialists. But it can be demonstrated that in the farm states of the Middle West and South, demands popularized by the Populists gained wide acceptance in later years. To claim that the Populists were the main cause of the twentieth-century Progressive movement is to claim too much, but this extravagant claim has been advanced by those who have not studied Populism in depth rather than by those who have.

The influence that one movement has on a subsequent movement usually is an intriguing subject. Most movements are the composite of many influences, and the Populists and Progressives were no exceptions. The Populists did make their contributions to Progressivism in much the same spirit that the Grangers, the Farmers Alliancemen, and others made their contributions to the Populists. The Populist contribution was mostly felt in the agricultural states of the Middle West and South. The Populists borrowed, edited, and stole planks from contemporary farmer groups in much the same fashion that the Progressives borrowed, edited, and stole planks from them and others.

Of late, surprise has been expressed that planks popularized by the Populists appeared in the programs of the Republicans and Democratic parties before the Populist Party was launched. It is difficult to understand why anyone who has studied the agrarian demands of the late nineteenth century would be surprised by such findings. These planks go to the very essence of the Populist Party. They are evidence of the abortive efforts of the pre-Populist agrarians who sought to obtain reforms by working from within one of the major parties. The farmer organizations that spearheaded the drive for legislative reforms deliberately chose to avoid forming a new party from fear that this would have a disruptive effect on the membership and the future of their organizations. Instead they confined themselves to drafting resolutions for consideration by one or both of the major parties. Prior to 1890 many of the politically oriented agrarians believed that one of the two major parties was sympathetic to them, but they were wrong.

Those who banded together to form the Populist Party had lost faith in the two major parties and in the promises of cooperative marketing and purchasing, better credit facilities, and improved farming methods to bring quick relief to the farmers. Political action, they argued, would deliver them from their oppressors in a shorter time. After launching the Populist Party, the politically motivated agrarians and their allies incorporated into their platforms planks that previously had found their way into the platforms of the Republicans and Democrats. There wasn't anything mysterious or secretive about who the Populists were. Many, if not most, of them were identified at one time or another with the contemporary farmer organizations. Keeping close tab on what these groups did is basic for an understanding of where the Populist Party came from and where it was heading. To deny the relevance of these important feeder groups is to deny the significance of a relevant phase of Populism.

Recently, we have been informed that the farmers were more receptive to the idea of a third party than was labor. In fact, we have

been assured, tentatively at least, that the agrarians wanted this coalition so badly that the reasons for its failure must be attributed to the conservative and retarding influence of labor. This, in my opinion, is questionable.

The views of a handful of politically active farmer and labor leaders who claimed they represented the sentiments of their respective organizations is hardly conclusive evidence. Editorial endorsements purporting to be representative of the choice of the farmers, as a rule, reflected the choices of the publishers or editors of these newspapers and not of the farmers. Rarely did the farmers have a voice in shaping editorial policies. Such papers usually were private property and not the property of the farm clubs or organizations. Substantial evidence based on primary source materials reflecting pro-labor attitudes on the part of a large number of rank-and-file farmers has not been produced to substantiate the view that the farmers were the more eager of the two to forge such a political coalition. I doubt whether such evidence will ever be produced. Farmer spokesmen frequently have been known to misrepresent the farmers as well as represent them. Resolutions were passed, it is true, heralding the formation of a farmer-labor alignment; fraternal greetings were exchanged between the two groups during their annual conventions, and these usually were applauded; the oppressors of the farmers and wage earners were denounced; and a new day based on farmer-labor cooperation was promised. But the truth of the matter is that nothing of lasting importance emerged from these testimonials.

At best, the pro-labor pronouncements of the Populist farmers were pronouncements of convenience and opportunism. A new party was launched. The support of labor was needed at the ballot box, and one way of getting this was by endorsing the demands of labor. In this instance, as in others before and after the Populists, the farmer-labor coalition was short-lived because a community of in-

terests between the farmers and wage earners
was lacking. Yet the effort to unite was made,
and this resulted in the incorporation into the
Populist platform of planks in favor of the
eight-hour day, government ownership of the
railroads, and other demands viewed as consistent with the best interests of labor.

Experiences bear out that the political flir-
tations between the farmers and wage earners
were brief. The Populist farmers no doubt felt
sorrow and sympathized with wage earners
exploited by a common foe—large corporations and "monopolies"—but these farmers
also considered themselves a cut or two better
than their erstwhile allies. Many, if not most,
farmers were property owners or potential
property owners who had a need for hired
labor. Their decisions were likely to be
guided by the size of their pocketbooks. Why
should these farmer-employers agitate for a
shorter work day and higher wages for hired
hands when this would mean higher production costs for them and higher prices for
many of the goods and services they bought?
Why should the wage-earner campaign for
the free and unlimited coinage of silver when
this was likely to mean higher prices for food,
clothing, and shelter? Exhortation was unlikely to resolve these conflicting interests.
Telling the farmers and wage earners ·that
they were both exploited by corporations,
bankers, and monopolists might have had a
temporary political appeal, but that is all. In
periods of acute economic distress, the
farmers and wage earners have been known
to come together and conduct successful campaigns, but these working conditions usually
disintegrated with the return of good times.
This is what happened to the Populists. The
role played by organized labor in the Populist
movement has been exaggerated. The only
group to support it was the Knights of Labor
which was well on the road to extinction,
while the emerging American Federation of
Labor avoided the Populists.

The question also has been raised as to
whether the Populist Party was a national or
sectional party. This is largely a matter of
definition and the counting of votes. If, by a
national party, one means a party that waged
vigorous contests and polled a substantial
number of votes in all sections of the country,
then one clearly is in the wrong in claiming
that the Populist Party was a national party,
for it was not. The vote-gathering abilities of
the Populists were poor in all states east of
Chicago. They polled most of their votes in
states in the Great Plains region, the South,
the Rocky Mountains, and the Far West. The
Populist Party might have been national on
paper and in thunder, but not in actuality. In
the presidential election of 1892, only
Nevada, Idaho, and Colorado gave more than
50 percent of their popular vote to Weaver,
the Populist candidate for president, while
the vote for the Bryan-Watson ticket in 1896
came as a grave disappointment to the Populists whose thunder had been stolen by the
Bryan-Sewall ticket.

Perhaps no argument has stirred more
comment than the revisionist charge that
Populism was a forerunner of American
fascism. The revisionists have stressed what
they considered were evidences of anti-
foreignism, anti-Semitism, conspiracy, and
the hatred of the international bankers which
one can easily link with the Nazis and fascists
of the 1930's. Hofstadter has refrained from
using the word "fascist," but some feel that he
inferred as much; Daniel Bell, on the other
hand, wrote that "the radical right of the
early 1960's is in no way different from the
Populist of the 1890's who for years traded
successfully on such simple formulas as 'Wall
Street,' 'international bankers' and 'the
Trusts'. . . ."

Most outspoken in his characterization of
Populism as a prototype of American fascism
was Victor Ferkiss, a political scientist whose
extreme position was accepted by few histo-

rians. Ferkiss left little doubt about his views when he wrote: ". . .movements such as those led by Huey Long, Father Coughlin, and Gerald L. K. Smith. . .were. . .the culmination of an ideological development stemming from such generally revered movements as Populism and 'agrarian democracy.' " He identifies some essential phases of Populism as features of fascism, such as a nationalistic program that was geared to appeal to the middle classes, an expressed hatred for the international bankers, and a declining faith in democratic institutions.

There is little to quarrel with the argument that the Populists appealed to the middle classes; for most movements, Populist and non-Populists alike, have had to promise something to the middle classes which usually furnish the backbone of a successful movement. Although we have no specific evidence how many of the farmers and townspeople who voted for the Populists were middle class property owners, the presumption is that it must have been a significant number. However, if appealing to the middle classes is a sign of fascism, we must be prepared to condemn a wide array of movements that many of us have considered a part of the American democratic tradition, including the American Federation of Labor, the Railroad Brotherhoods, the Progressives, most general farmer organizations, cooperative associations, farmer-labor parties, and third parties in general. One can find doses of anti-foreignism, anti-Semitism, patrioteering, and middle class appeal in the ranks of all these organizations.

Again, as for the nationalistic features, I believe that the revisionists have likewise overemphasized this. The Populists were no more and no less nationalistic in their orientation than rank-and-file Americans. The predominant interest in the domestic affairs of the nation and a secondary concern with what went on abroad is something that transcended party lines. The Republicans and Democrats at least equalled, if they did not exceed, the Populists in their nationalistic outlook, and the voters took them more seriously. After all, the Republican and Democratic parties were older parties and far more successful at the ballot box. If nationalism was one of the cornerstones of fascism, then the American people of the 1890's, as a whole, should shoulder the blame for entertaining such thoughts—not the Populists alone.

There is little evidence to support the contention that the Populists were losing faith in democratic institutions; if anything, the evidence points in the opposite direction: the Populists fought to broaden the social, political, and economic base of democracy and not to restrict it. For how else can one explain their agitation in behalf of the secret ballot, direct election of United States senators, the income tax, woman suffrage, and related demands. They wanted to correct the imbalance in government at all levels by giving the farmers, the small merchants, and the mechanics the representation they believed were deserved. To argue that the Populists were incapable of grasping the significance of independence because they failed to produce a comprehensive document on "human freedom or the fuller life" is unconvincing. The Populists drafted various documents and resolutions that were geared to immediate action. Like most Americans, they were long on action and short on theory, but they knew what they were after.

As for the distrust of the international bankers, I think that this, too, has been overstated. If anything, the "international bankers" theme was brought up much less frequently in Populist propaganda than complaints against the eastern banking interests. The airing of such grievances had been part of the American tradition of dissent.

Many of the colonists believed that the monied interests conspired to keep them in a perpetual state of bondage to Great Britain. Andrew Jackson and his followers were equally distrustful of the bankers, but somehow or other they and the colonists have been spared the onus of being branded as fascists.

I believe that the revisionists would be on much safer ground if they argued that the Populists included some individuals who, by 1930 standards, manifested certain fascistic tendencies. David Saposs agreed with this view in his perceptive essay on "The Role of the Middle Classes in Social Development." Writing in 1935 when the academic interest in the role of the middle classes was growing and facism was a real threat, Saposs classified members of the Populist tradition into three categories.

The first category contained those who rallied around the League for Independent Political Action headed by Professor John Dewey of Columbia University. Dewey, of course, was no agrarian; still in the early 1930's Dewey expressed the same lack of faith in the two major parties that the Populists of the 1890's voiced and urged the formation of a third party with a far-reaching program of social control. But, unlike the Populists, the Dewey group was militantly international and said little that could be interpreted as nationalistic or fascistic.

A second and more substantial Populist-oriented group during the 1930's consisted of Robert M. La Follette, Jr., George W. Norris, Lynn Frazier, Gerald P. Nye, Burton K. Wheeler, and Fiorello LaGuardia. This faction had the Railroad Brotherhoods and most of the unions in the American Federation of Labor as allies; it agitated for government operation of Muscle Shoals and other public utilities and fought for tax reforms that would lighten the burden of the poor man. This group followed the liberal-nationalist line of the Populists and was isola-

tionist in foreign policy, but its nationalism was nonchauvinistic and nonjingoistic. Phil La Follette organized a third party in 1938 which many were convinced had fascistic overtones, and he did this much against the wishes of his brother Bob who opposed Franco's Spain and suffered at the ballot box as a consequence. Needless to say, Phil La Follette's third party was never accepted by the voters of Wisconsin and the nation.

The third Populist type of the 1930's which, in my opinion, was semi-fascistic, was found in the South and Southwest; this element represented a form of political extremism and perhaps came closest to what the revisionists had in mind. Most representative of this group was Huey Long whose hatred for big business interests exceeded his dislike of the Negroes whose votes he openly solicited. He appealed to the small businessmen, the "hill-billies," and the poor whites of the rural and urban areas. Huey Long and his type differed remarkably from the more stable and less provincial elements that inherited the mantle of Populism in the Middle West.

However, the threats of fascism came more from the urban than the rural elements during the 1930's. As examples, one can cite the "Khaki Shirts," an offshoot of the Bonus Expeditionary Forces, Father Cox's "Blue Shirts" and "Hunger Marchers," Dudley Pelley's "Silver Shirts," the German-American Bund, the followers of Father Charles Coughlin, certain elements in the American Legion, and other splinter groups.

Most Populists, even in the South, simply do not fall into this fascist category. The Populists sought the Negro vote and urged the Negro to join the party on the premise that the forces of monopoly did not respect race, color, or creed. The Populists were the victims of the mob spirit and intolerance, not the proponents of it. To be a Populist in the South required real courage, and the penalty for succumbing to its subversive doctrines was greater in the states of the old Confederacy than it was in the North. Populism placed greater stress on social and economic issues than on the race question and thus held out the prospect of racial equality which was tantamount to heresy. The Populists by threatening the one-party system were repudiating everything that most Southerners considered decent in society.

These are not signs of the loss of faith in the democratic process as has been suggested by at least one revisionist, but of tolerance and a determination to strengthen the democratic process. Once the "back of Populism was broken," the "black belt whites," the most vigorous foes of the third party, solidified their position, and recruited "enough upcountry support to adopt poll taxes, literacy tests, and other instruments to disfranchise the Negro." In fact this began with the Mississippi Constitutional Convention of 1890 before Populism reached its peak and continued until new constitutions were adopted by seven states from 1895 to 1910. "Understanding clauses" and the white primary provisions of constitutions and laws were of major importance in reducing the number of votes. Populism, by threatening white supremacy, backfired and strengthened the one-party system.

The money question remained a reformist issue well after the disintegration of the Populist Party in the late 1890's. In mid-April 1933, for example, sixteen of the forty or more inflationary bills pending in Congress sought the purchase of silver, the increase of silver certificates, or bimetallism at the ratio of 16 to 1. In the initial stages of the New Deal, no other proposal inspired as many money bills as the one advocated by the Populists.

The Populist argument has even haunted the post-World War II generation. In fact, the monetary views of Milton Friedman, professor of economics at the University of Chicago and one of the leading classical econ-omists and theoreticians, whose name was linked with Senator Barry Goldwater's during the presidential campaign of 1964, sound very similar to those of the Populists. Friedman, if I understand him correctly, argues that "the key to capitalistic economic stability is monetary policy—the factors that govern the rate of growth or decline in the money supply." This, it appears to me, was the crux of the Populist argument and suggests that Populism has acquired respectability in the very institution of higher learning in which it was denounced by one of the foremost critics of the 1890's.

Friedman's book, *A Monetary History of the United States, 1867 to 1960*, which he co-authored with Anna J. Schwartz and published in 1962 under the auspices of the National Bureau of Economic Research, is most useful. The policy of the Bureau prohibits the formulation of specific policy conclusions, and Friedman and Schwartz made none. But, in reading between the lines and what has been written elsewhere, one cannot help concluding that Friedman is saying that the requisite of stable economic growth is stable monetary growth. This is putting the Populist argument of the 1890's in an academic attire of the 1960's. The Populists maintained that the whole of industry, agriculture, and commerce could not be set in complete motion and the economic health of the nation restored unless the money supply kept pace with the growth of population and all other sectors of the economy. In the 1890's this was a hairbrained notion that a bunch of money cranks were trying to foist on the nation; in the 1960's one of today's foremost conservative economists is advocating that the money supply of the country be increased at a rate of from three to five percent annually. Times and needs have changed, but this goes beyond what the Populists proposed when they demanded an increase in the supply of money until it reached fifty dollars per capita. The Populist proposal, it seems to me, was mild compared to what Friedman is suggesting.

How successful have the revisionists been in bringing about an acceptance of their views and in causing a re-evaluation of the standard interpretation of Populism? Not very successful, in my opinion. They have stimulated a lot of discussion and rekindled fresh interest in Populism, which is a very commendable contribution. But, as yet, no scholar who has accepted the revisionist position has come forward with a full-scale study buttressing their arguments. Curiously enough, those who have taken the revisionists most seriously have been some of the sociologists.

John Hicks has remained quiet for the most part and has not answered the revisionists directly, but he has had something to say about this general topic. In 1956 Hicks published "Our Pioneer Heritage: A Reconsideration" in which he re-appraised an earlier article that appeared in the *Prairie Schooner* in 1928 and which contained much of the thinking that later went into *The Populist Revolt.* "It wasn't a bad article," wrote Hicks some twenty-eight years later. "Nevertheless, I shouldn't care to have it republished in its original form, for if I were writing on the same subject today I wouldn't say the same things. . . ." He concedes that, when ' he wrote in 1928, he was under the spell of Frederick Jackson Turner and that he tried "to make our pioneer background explain far more than it could explain." Hicks felt that he had good reason for writing as he did in 1928; as a young schoolteacher in Johnson County, Wyoming, Hicks had seen "authentic remnants" of the last American frontier. At the time he wrote this and *The Populist Revolt,* he lived in Nebraska which only recently had passed through the frontier process. It was easy for him and his students, as he says, to magnify their experiences. Hicks assured his readers that he was not turning his back on Turner, and that, if he were writing on the same theme in 1956, he would not have ignored the frontier influence. He would, however, have placed more emphasis on the effects of the industrial revolution, urban life, and the relations between the United States and the rest of the world.

To me the impact of the industrial revolution on agriculture is a subject of primary importance, although it should not cause us to dismiss the frontier influence as inconsequential. It was not a matter of the frontier or the industrial revolution, but of both. The frontier, used in its broadest context, besides contributing to certain attitudes about money, railroads, and trusts, resulted in the throwing open of large quantities of land that contributed to our agricultural surpluses. This influenced the complexion of our economy. The farmers of nineteenth-century America provided raw materials and foodstuffs for the urban populations and industries of Western Europe at ridiculously low prices and thus hastened the industrialization of that part of the world. By selling our agricultural surpluses abroad, the United States obtained cash and credit and the technical know-how that speeded up our own industrialization. This, in turn, lessened our dependence on Europe for manufactured products and the Europeans retaliated by purchasing their agricultural needs elsewhere. The basic contributions of the farmers to the industrialization of America and the effect this had on our foreign market for agricultural products is a story that historians have yet to tell.

Much of this went on under the noses of the Populists who were too close to it to recognize its significance. Industry was reaching maturity. The complexion of our capitalist society was changing and a profound effect exerted on agriculture. This dynamic industrial capitalism displayed an insatiable appetite for innovations and material progress that upset the equilibrium and ushered in changes in production, distribution, and social values that the tradition-bound farmers did not understand. In the process, agriculture which had long been heralded as "the noblest and most deserving" of occupations was relegated to a subordinate position in society. Farmers who were unable to make the necessary adjustments to the emerging industrial order and were a part of agriculture that was becoming more and more commercialized were forced deeper and deeper into debt and eventually out of farming.

Then, too, more stress needs to be placed on the agrarian proposals that were obscured by the more popular demands for monetary, railroad, and land legislation reforms. For instance, during the 1880's and the 1890's, agitation was waged to curtail the output of tobacco and cotton as a means of strengthening the position of the producers in the market place. This agitation mounted during the 1890's and the first decade of the twentieth century and helped prepare the Southerners for the New Deal. The effectiveness of these campaigns may be rightfully questioned, but the fact that they were waged cannot be denied.

To me it also appears that the agrarian demands for the income tax have been treated in too perfunctory a fashion by historians. This is a subject of the first magnitude. It is inadequate to state that the Populists and their agrarian forebears agitated for the income tax. The agrarians were the most insistent and the most active of the income tax pioneers—more so than the members of other occupational groups and the Socialists—in emphasizing the inequalities in the tax structure that placed a disproportionate share of the tax burden on the landowning farmers. The far-reaching effects of the income tax were not appreciated in nineteenth-century America as they are today. Historians would do well to re-examine in depth the relations of the late nineteenth-century agrarians to the

income tax and recast the subject in the light which I believe it deserves.

The illiberal phases of Populism have been overlooked, but these, in my opinion, did not consist of anti-foreignism, anti-Semitism, and a loss of faith in democratic institutions. Some intolerance existed, but not to the extent that the revisionists would have us believe. One can cite interference with academic freedom, as at Kansas State College, Manhattan, where the Board of Regents controlled by the Populists interfered with curriculum offerings and faculty appointments. Academic freedom was not as carefully defined during the 1890's, and groups other than the Populists engaged in practices that would be repulsive to liberals of today.

Nor should one overlook some of the less flattering aspects of the Populists. They attracted their fair share of grafters, crooks, and opportunists who were much more interested in advancing their personal fortunes than in alleviating the plight of the farmers. These unsavory characters did irreparable harm to the Populist cause and to later efforts to organize the farmers along social and economic lines. The extent to which such individuals managed to infiltrate the ranks of the Populists is unknown, but that they did cannot be disputed.

Whatever one thinks of the revisionist arguments in seeking to bring about a re-evaluation of the Populists, they have helped revive an interest in Populism. The hope now is that the revisionists themselves and those who have taken them to heart will sit down and do some research with primary sources. Perhaps then they will come forward with fresh and abundant evidence that will bear out their contentions, but so far they have failed to do this. The preponderance of evidence is with the standard interpretation. Scholars of the post-World War II era such as Stuart Noblin, author of *Leonidas Lafayette Polk*, Martin Ridge, the biographer of *Ignatius Donnelly*, and others, including Norman Pollack (with whose analysis in *The Populist Response to Industrial America* I disagree sharply) and Walter T. K. Nugent, the author of *The Tolerant Populists,* lend additional weight to the constructive features of Populism that Hicks stressed. What we know about Populism we owe chiefly to Hicks' efforts and those of other scholars of the pre- and post-World War II eras who have worked diligently and patiently with the primary sources.

Suggested Readings

Secondary materials dealing with Populism are more plentiful than most students realize, but not as abundant as they should be. Heading the list is John D. Hicks's influential *The Populist Revolt* (Minneapolis, 1931), which still is the most valuable work in the field. Another analytical and sympathetic study is Roscoe C. Martin, *The People's Party in Texas* (Austin, 1933). Recent scholarly works that also treat Populism in a similarly friendly spirit are: Walter T. K. Nugent, *The Tolerant Populists* (Chicago, 1963) and Norman Pollack, *The Populist Response to Industrial America* (Cambridge, Mass., 1962). Two recent publications are: Robert F. Durden, *The Climax of Populism* (Lexington, Ky., 1965), which presents a new interpretation of the election of 1896, and George B. Tindall (ed.), *A Populist Reader* (New York, 1966), which contains a helpful collection of contemporary articles, essays, and excerpts on Populism.

Contemporary accounts of a primary character which view Populism in a socially constructive light are: N. B. Ashby, *The Riddle of the Sphinx* (Des Moines, 1890); T. W. Scott Morgan, *History of the Wheel and Alliance* (Fort Scott, Kan., 1889); and, by a prominent political spokesman, William A. Peffer, *The Farmer's Side* (New York, 1891). Frank LeRond McVey, *The Populist Movement* (New York, 1896) is a critical appraisal.

Pertinent background material will be found in: Fred A. Shannon, *The Farmer's Last Frontier* (New York, 1945); Solon J. Buck, *The Granger Movement* (Cambridge, Mass., 1913); and Theodore Saloutos, *Farmer Movements in the South, 1865–1933* (Berkeley and Los Angeles, 1960). See also Theodore Saloutos, "The Agricultural Problem and Nineteenth-Century Industrialism," *Agricultural History*, XXII (July, 1948), 156–174. A provocative series of essays has been brought together by Chester M. Destler in *American Radicalism, 1865–1901* (Menasha, Wis., 1946). Lawrence J. Laughlin, "Causes of Agricultural Unrest," *Atlantic Monthly*, LXXVIII (November, 1896), 577–585, is by a prominent scholar of the conservative persuasion. More recent accounts are: Charles Hoffmann, "The Depression of the Nineties," *Journal of Economic History*, XVI (June, 1956), 137–164, and Samuel Rezneck, "Unemployment, Unrest, Relief in the United States during the Depression of 1893–1897," *Journal of Political Economy*, LXI (August, 1953), 324–345.

Two recent accounts of the election of 1896 are: Paul Glad, *The Trumpet Soundeth* (Lincoln, Nebr., 1961) and Stanley L. Jones, *The Presidential Election of 1896* (Madison, Wis., 1964). Suggestive is William Diamond, "Urban and Rural Voting in 1896," *American Historical Review*, XLVI (January, 1941), 281–305. Broader in scope are: Horace S. Merrill, *Bourbon Democracy of the Middle West, 1865–1896* (Baton Rouge, 1896) and J. Rogers Hollingsworth, *The Whirligig of Politics* (Chicago, 1963).

Regional and local monographs of Populism are numerous for the southern states. A pioneering work is Alex M. Arnett, *The Populist Movement in Georgia* (New York, 1922), which can be read profitably in conjunction with Robert P. Brooks, *The Agrarian Revolution in Georgia, 1865–1912* (Madison, Wis., 1914). Other local studies are: John B. Clark, *Populism in Alabama* (Auburn, Ala., 1927); Albert D. Kirwan, *Revolt of the Rednecks* (Lexington, Ky., 1951); Daniel M. Robison, *Bob Taylor and the Agrarian Revolt in Tennessee* (Chapel Hill, N.C., 1935); and W. DuBose Sheldon, *Populism in the Old Dominion* (Princeton, N.J., 1935).

Good biographical studies of Populist leaders include: C. Vann Woodward, *Tom Watson: Agrarian Rebel* (New York, 1938), available also in paperback edition; Martin Ridge, *Ignatius Don-*

nelly (Chicago, 1962); Stuart Noblin, *Leonidas LaFayette Polk* (Chapel Hill, N.C., 1949); Francis B. Simpkins, *Pitchfork Ben Tillman* (Baton Rouge, 1944); and Frederick E. Haynes, *James Baird Weaver* (Iowa City, 1919). Three of these volumes are concerned with southern agrarian leaders.

Scholarly treatments of Populism in the South include: Hallie Farmer, "The Economic Background of Southern Populism," *South Atlantic Quarterly*, XXIX (January, 1930), 77–91; Benjamin J. Kendrick, "Agrarian Discontent in the South, 1880–1900," *American Historical Association Report 1920* (Washington, 1925), 265–272; Alex M. Arnett, "The Populist Movement in Georgia," *Georgia Historical Quarterly*, VII (December, 1923), 313–338; John D. Hicks, "The Farmers' Alliance in North Carolina," *North Carolina Historical Review*, II (April, 1925), 162–187; Kathryn T. Abbey, "Florida Versus the Principles of Populism," *Journal of Southern History*, IV (November, 1938), 462–475; Lucia E. Daniel, "The Louisiana People's Party," *Louisiana Historical Quarterly*, XXVI (October, 1943), 1055–1149; James O. Knauss, "The Farmers' Alliance in Florida," *South Atlantic Quarterly*, XXV (July, 1926), 300–315; and Ralph Smith, "The Farmers' Alliance in Texas, 1875–1900," *Southwestern Historical Quarterly*, XLVIII (January, 1945), 346–369. The business aspects of the movement are discussed in Ralph Smith, " 'Macuneism,' or the Farmers of Texas in Business." *Journal of Southern History*, XIII (May, 1947), 220–244 and Fred A. Shannon, "C. W. Macune and the Farmers' Alliance," *Current History*, XXVIII (June, 1955), 330–335.

Helpful articles dealing with Populism and its antecedents, and written primarily during the 1920s, are: Ernest D. Stewart, "The Populist Party in Indiana," *Indiana Magazine of History*, XIV (December, 1918), 332–367, and *Indiana Magazine of History*, XV (March, 1919), 53–74; John D. Hicks, "The Origin and Early History of the Farmers' Alliance in Minnesota," *Mississippi Valley Historical Review*, IX (December, 1922), 203–226, and "The People's Party in Minnesota," *Minnesota Historical Bulletin*, V (November, 1924), 531–560; Herman C. Nixon, "The Economic Basis of the Populist Movement

in Iowa," *Iowa Journal of History and Politics*, XXI (July, 1923), 373–396, and "The Populist Movement in Iowa," *Iowa Journal of History and Politics*, XXIV (January, 1926), 3–107. Raymond C. Miller writes about "The Background of Populism in Kansas" in *Mississippi Valley Historical Review*, XI (March, 1925), 469–489. Still other phases of Populism are discussed by Halle Farmer, "The Economic Background of Frontier Populism," *Mississippi Valley Historical Review*, XIII (December, 1926), 387–397; John D. Barnhart, "Rainfall and the Populist Party in Nebraska," *American Political Science Review*, XIX (August, 1925), 527–540; and John D. Hicks, "The Birth of the Populist Party," *Minnesota History*, IX (September, 1928), 219–248. Also helpful is Leon W. Fuller, "Colorado's Revolt Against Capitalism," *Mississippi Valley Historical Review*, XXI (December, 1934), 343–360. An interpretative approach by John D. Hicks is "Some Parallels with Populism in the Twentieth Century," *Social Education*, VIII (November, 1944), 297–301.

An important but little stressed subject is dealt with by Jack Abramowitz in two articles: "The Negro in the Agrarian Revolt," *Agricultural History*, XXIV (April, 1950), 89–95, and "The Negro in the Populist Movement," *Journal of Negro History*, XXXVIII (July, 1953), 257–289. Earlier studies are those by Francis B. Simkins, "Ben Tillman's View of the Negro," *Journal of Southern History*, III (May, 1937), 161–174, and C. Vann Woodward, "Tom Watson and the Negro," *Journal of Southern History*, IV (February, 1938), 14–33. Also suggestive is Gunnar Myrdahl, *An American Dilemma* (New York, 1944), 452–455.

Revisionist interpretations and reactions are found in: Paul S. Holbo, "Wheat or What? Populism and American Fascism," *Western Political Quarterly*, XIV (September, 1961), 727–736, and William P. Tucker, "Ezra Pound, Fascism and Populism," *Journal of Politics*, XVIII (February, 1956), 105–107. Reactions against the revisionists are available in Norman Pollack, "The Myth of Populist Anti-Semitism," *American Historical Review*, LXVIII (October, 1962), 76–80, and "Hofstadter on Populism: A Critique of 'The Age of Reform,' " *Journal of Southern History*, XXVI (November, 1960), 478–500. An especially perceptive answer to the revisionists is in Walter T. K. Nugent, *The Tolerant Populists* (Chicago, 1963), 231–243.

Three phases of Populism are discussed by: George H. Knoles, "Populism and Socialism with Special Reference to the Election of 1892," *Pacific Historical Review*, XII (September, 1943), 295–304; J. L. Colwell, "Populist Image of Vernon L. Parrington," *Mississippi Valley Historical Review*, XLIX (June, 1962), 52–56; and Martin J. Klotsche, "The 'United Front' Populists," *Wisconsin Magazine of History*, II (June, 1937), 275–389.

Conflicting views on the origins of the controversial subtreasury plan will be found in John D. Hicks, "The Sub-Treasury: A Forgotten Plan for the Relief of Agriculture," *Mississippi Valley Historical Review*, XV (December, 1928), 355–373

and James C. Malin, "The Farmers' Alliance Subtreasury Plan and European Precedents," *Mississippi Valley Historical Review,* XXXI (September, 1944), 255–260. Compare Theodore Saloutos, *Farmer Movements in the South, 1865–1933* (Berkeley and Los Angeles, 1960), 119–122, 135, and 138.

Recent articles on Populism include: Norman Pollack, "Fear of Man: Populism, Authoritarianism, and the Historian," *Agricultural History*, XXXIX (April, 1965), 59–67; Oscar Handlin, "Reconsidering the Populists," *Agricultural History*, XXXIX, 68–74; Irwin Unger, "Critique of Norman Pollack's 'Fear of Man,' " *Agricultural History*, XXXIX, 75–80; and J. Rogers Hollingsworth, "Populism: The Problem of Rhetoric and Reality," *Agricultural History*, XXXIX, 81–85.